Stephen King's America

Stephen King's America

Jonathan P. Davis

Bowling Green State University Popular Press
Bowling Green, OH 43403

Library of Congress Catalogue Card No.: 93-73797

ISBN: 0-87972-647-4 Clothbound
        0-87972-648-2 Paperback

Cover art by Paul Faris

Cover design by Dumm Art

ACKNOWLEDGEMENTS

Before we begin to explore Stephen King's America, I wish to acknowledge the several people whose contributions and inspirations made the journey possible:

My mother and father, John and Barbara Davis, whose undying support of me gave birth to the perseverance needed to complete projects such as this one.

My brothers, Christopher and Andrew, who both tolerate (sometimes) the sound of a computer keyboard in the late hours of the night and who are enthusiastic about Stephen King because of my enthusiasm.

Courtney Gardner, who had been there through thick and thin with support and all the right suggestions.

My buddy, Joe Arrigo, my partner in horror-fiction gluttony.

North Central College, Naperville, Illinois, for having the open-mindedness to reward such a project with scholarship funds.

Dr. Fran Navakas, who through her guidance and willingness to knead through the stacks of manuscript is as much a part of this as I am.

Shirley Sonderegger, Stephen King's secretary, whose hospitality and friendly role as go-between made corresponding with the King office a great pleasure.

Tony Magistrale, whose zeal for my project prompted him to invite me out to Vermont to participate in his class, swap ideas, and conduct an interview (Thanks Tony!).

Carroll Terrell, who gave a great interview and plenty of laughs.

Burton Hatlen, for his great insight and interest in my project.

Gary Hoppenstand, a gentleman and a scholar, whose contribution and excitement for Stephen King's fiction has spawned a meaningful friendship.

The late Ted Dikty, Starmont House, whose interest during the initial drafting stages provided the catalyst.

Bowling Green State University Popular Press, the medium that brought my passion for the subject to fruition.

And finally, Stephen King, whose love for life and writing has given me the greatest inspiration of all.

CONTENTS

FOREWORD

I remember my interest in Stephen King beginning at a garage sale one sunny August afternoon in 1979. I was pawing through a rack of dirty, used hardcover books for fifty cents each. After dismissing most of them, I noticed a grungy-looking gray book that looked like it hadn't been touched in years. I picked it up and held it. After taking in the simplicity of its exterior (it lacked a dust jacket), I began to flip through the pages. I didn't have time to really sample the piece, but the titles caught my attention: "Jerusalem's Lot," "I Am the Doorway," "Graveyard Shift," "The Mangler." At the time, I had already been a die-hard horror fan, having previously terrified myself with the pages of William Peter Blatty's *The Exorcist* and David Seltzer's *The Omen,* among others that dominated the paperback racks across America at the time. I had heard of Stephen King before because of the movie *Carrie,* but I'd never read a single one of his works. After taking in the stories' titles, I turned over the fifty and took it home nested underneath my arm. The book was called *Night Shift.*

Over the next couple of weeks, I read the book, jumping from story to story randomly. I didn't read it all; what I did read was enough. I was taken into a world where a lawn-care service representative terrorizes his clients; where children overthrow the adult population through bloodshed and turn their allegiance to a god who lives in a Nebraska cornfield; to a rural Maine town where vampires of past nightmares come back to prey on a family from out of town. To the young mind scratching the door of adolescence, these stories were ample to create a flurry of nightmares. Yet at the same time those stories caused mental unease, they had a strong magnetic appeal. The author of those stories seemed to possess an uncanny ability to focus on ordinary individuals and place them in extraordinary circumstances, ones which were filled with horror. It was at that time in my life when I began to realize the appeal of dread and the compulsion it bred in my mind. After I'd read several stories in the book, I once again wanted to know what hid underneath my

1

bed; I wanted to know if there was a maggot-infested decaying hand ready to reach through the crack in my closet door. It was after reading those stories that I became convinced that I was dealing with a man who knew how to scare me, and I appreciated him for it. After all, is not fear one of the most accepted characteristics of being human? Fear serves some of the most vital functions of survival; without it, we would be lost. Is it not fear that keeps us from sticking our hands into a pot of boiling water? Is it not fear that makes us stick to lighted areas when walking home alone? Fear leaves us uneasy, overanxious, yet it saves us. It is one of the foundations of wisdom. Stephen King knows fear, and he knows that fear is not limited to any one group of people; it affects man, woman, or child as well as it reaches its icy cold fingers to black, white and Hispanic. While we as individuals may boast characteristics that differentiate us from our brothers and sisters, we all inevitably dip into the same well when we look into our rear view mirrors when driving alone at night and notice that a car has been following us too long to be coincidence. It is that same fear that keeps us driving, unwilling to pull over or get out of our cars, minimizing the risk of being harmed.

After that initial introduction to the fictional world of Stephen King, I took a few years off in favor of the football field and high school dances. After graduation, however, I began to pick up books at a quick pace once again. Need I tell you which books I went for first?

I have to admit that the emotion that took me back to Stephen King's books was the same one that prompted me to purchase that grungy-looking gray book that summer afternoon years before: the delight of dread. Only then, after eight more years of education and maturity, I had also turned to him for different reasons. The dark delight I received from fear was there as always, but now it was something more. I began to realize as I churned through book after book that I was dealing with much more than a man who could tell a scary tale. I was dealing with a man who understood the human condition on all levels. I was dealing with a man who found a comfortable fictional world right underneath his own two feet, which stood on the sacred ground of America; a man whose feelings about his country resonated throughout his fiction, adding an extra dimension to the horror that established the works as having a substance I'd not recognized before in my childish approach. But what I must point out is that it was good that I had read him from that childhish perspective, the one that cared only for the goosepimples that a really scary story could provide. King's fiction is valuable on several levels: it allows us to regress to a time when rationality took a back seat to the unknown, but it also allows the maturing mind to step back and take a look at the world, at the role morality plays in one's life, at one's relationship with technology, at becoming an adult, at surviving in a world that means to subordinate the individual in favor of a collective society. When we enter King's world, we are embarking on a tour of the human experience, one which takes us through all the phases of physical and mental development.

Stephen King has indeed built his reputation around the horror story. He has written in other genres for temporary vacations from his main domain, but he has admitted that he always returns from those vacations back home, where the evil awaits, to the work of horror. King has been asked often why it is that he chose horror over other forms of literature. His reaction is typically "What do you expect me to do?" After all, we live in a world of horrors where the ten o'clock news competes in content with the Saturday night creature feature. All one needs to do is glance at the front page of the newspaper or flip on the television to get a good dose of carnage: rape, murder, airplane crashes, gang violence, mob action, terrorist attacks. No matter where people turn their attention, they cannot go one single day with their eyes and ears open without learning of some new atrocity. Perhaps the reason why King turned to horror, why so many authors have recently turned to horror, it that it is subtextually a realist portrayal of life, only hidden behind masks, capes, and fangs. Perhaps the reason why millions of readers have turned to horror is because they have to. King addresses this in his foreword to *Night Shift*: "Life is full of horrors small and large, but because the small ones are the ones we can comprehend, they are the ones that smack home with all the force of mortality" (11). In a world where horrors equal to or worse than those written are a reality, it becomes essential to find that outlet, the one the horror novel provides, to escape into a world somewhat similar where the reader is safe and the protagonist has a chance to survive, often unlike the real world.

King understands the function of horror fiction, and he uses it to his advantage. His love for the spooky tales he absorbed from books and EC comics as a child has spread out to include his mature perspective on living, which has been enough to produce nearly thirty works of fiction in the field. As his inventory proves, one cannot dispute that he is perhaps one of the most productive minds of our generation. Not only does he write about things that are appealing in their creativity and pertinence to American life, but he has also proved himself as having an imagination that refuses to run dry. In a time where the spectrum of entertainment has had to regurgitate old material in its failure to find fresh, original concepts, a man like Stephen King should be welcomed with open arms. I'll tell you why.

First, he cares. About you. About me. He cares about the human condition that is the foundation of everything that happens in his stories. He utilizes popular culture appeal to make his books fun for us to read, but if people take the time to read into the subtexts of his fiction, they will find that he is trying to tell us much, much more. On the surface, his books are about such phenomenon as vampires, killer cars, haunted houses, pyrokinetics, telepathics. Yet, underneath the manifest, the true horrors stem from human misconduct: child abuse, alcoholism, self-serving governments, immoral sexual behavior, repressive societal organizations, and the distorted attitudes bred by societal expectations. We would be so lucky if other figures in the limelight of popular culture should be so concerned.

Second, he urges people of all ages to pick up a book and actually read. In an age where the television shapes our view of society, where stereotypes reign, educating our young and our old to view others simplistically, reading has taken a back seat. The idea of picking up a book and actually reading it is to many young people these days the equivalent of sweeping the garage on a sunny Saturday afternoon when their buddies want them to play ball. King's stories appeal to the masses, and therefore should be seen as a source of inspiration to a generation that has become less and less concerned with literacy and more concerned with generating wealth and popping movies into VCRs.

As these qualities of King's function in modern literature became more apparent, my excitement for what he was doing became too large to contain. My zeal for his work prompted me to propose a research project centered around travelling to his home base, Maine, where I would study his life and read the volumes of work he has donated to his alma mater, the University of Maine at Orono. North Central College, located in Naperville, Illinois, took up this proposal and gave me the money to perform the study.

After I had arrived in Maine, and calmed down, I picked up my rental car at Bangor International and drove to the university where I set up my lodgings.

During my first full day in Maine, something happened to me that perhaps put everything into perspective as to why I was there. As soon as the sun popped up from underneath the eastern horizon, I hopped in the rental car and drove out to take a look at King's house on West Broadway near downtown Bangor. I pulled up in front of the house and then parked two houses down (I didn't want to look too much like a tourist, although I'm sure I failed in my attempt at subtlety). I snatched my camera from the front passenger seat and approached.

I had been hoping that I would be the only one there so that I could take in the experience without magnifying my tourist appearance as one of many gawking at the millionaire's house, but I was not alone. There was a woman taking snapshots of it. I looked behind me and saw a man and two children sitting in an idling compact car. I looked back at her.

"Oh! I'm so glad you're here!" she said to me.

"Really?" I said.

"Yes," she said. "At least I'm not the only lunatic standing here gaping at his house!"

I laughed.

"I'm from Boston," she said.

"I'm from near Chicago," I replied.

We took a few pictures. Moments later, she said: "I love Stephen King. I have all of his books in hardback, and I won't let anyone touch them."

Well, that pretty much summed it up for me; what I was doing there, that is. Stephen King trips some live wire deep in the hearts of his reading public in a way that cannot be compared to other popular artists. He calls to us, he speaks our language, he shares our problems. He understands who we are. At that precise moment, I wondered if he really understood how those two people standing on his front lawn felt about him. I wonder if, in his celebrity status that has forced him to separate himself from the general public, he is beyond understanding or even caring. But I think if he could have stepped outside and talked to us, it would have become apparent to him that he has touched people he doesn't even know in a unique way.

I suppose another reason that I chose to travel to Maine to do my research rather than just labor in the nearest public library was because I wanted to feel Maine. I wanted to know the place that has had such a profound effect on King's writing. After all, one can seldom pick up a King book and not find a region of Maine inserted somewhere in the story. I also wanted to know why he picked that state (a state which, until he made it conspicuous through his inclusion of it in his writing, was to me, a Midwesterner, just another spot on the map) to live in: a state that removes him from the throbbing industrial entertainment centers of New York and Los Angeles. After spending two weeks there, I could tell why.

Maine is unlike any other state I've visited. Its landscapes are breathtaking. The smell of paper mills permeates the air. A lake, stream, or oceanic area is within short driving distance of most cultivated regions. But what I learned about Maine as to why King has set his hooks there I found in the people. They are very much to themselves, and they treat him like they would the carpenter from next door. They know who he is, all right, but they keep to their own business. King, unlike many celebrities now participating in America's entertainment scene, has the liberty of leaving his house without armed guards. He keeps the gates to his house open. There is no barbed wire at the top of his fence. I believe his townfolk treat him this way because they sincerely take pride in having him there and want to keep him there. After all, how many residents of small cities can boast of having a worldwide celebrity as a neighbor?

When I boarded the plane home, however, I think what hit me most about being in Maine and knowing that King lives in Maine is that it put into crystal-clear perspective the fact that King is American. He lives in a state that was a part of the original thirteen colonies, where the logging industry has reigned for two centuries, where the majority of men and women do not walk around in pinstriped suits carrying briefcases on their way to towering skyscrapers. King is a living, breathing part of a unique region of this country, a region that in its uniqueness basically sums up the human condition in America. America is not a homogenous country but rather takes pride in its diversity of people and landscapes. I think it is King's realization that he inhabits a mere portion of the larger whole that may perhaps have one of the largest influences on his fiction. Living in Maine, King is able to experience his humanity as his sensory input from his surroundings dictates to him, yet he also has the freedom to travel outside of his region to taste the vastness of this country and its varying forms of people and geography.

One can look at King as not only a creative navigator of the American terrain but also as an appendage of the American literary tradition he's inherited. All one needs to do is open up any American literature anthology to find an array of authors who all were greatly influenced by their regions: Mark Twain, Flannery O'Connor, William Faulkner, H.P. Lovecraft, Nathaniel Hawthorne. Yet while King and his literary predecessors are differentiated by their regional flavors, they all seem to be able to grasp the concept that while America is unique in its variety of regions, the people who inhabit those regions all dip into the same pool of human vulnerability. Landscape may affect the way an individual views the world physically, but when it comes down to the bone, each and every American is equipped with universal trials and concerns. King's link to his American predecessors is evident if one can step back and make the parallels. King writes about children and the tumultuous period of life known as adolescence; he writes about the traumas that produce coming-of-age and rites of passage. Mark Twain repeatedly wrote about the same things: *Huckleberry Finn, Tom Sawyer.* King writes about the disintegration of the family and the retreat of human beings into lonely isolation. William Faulkner wrote recurringly of the same subjects, most notably in *As I Lay Dying.* King writes about the fanatical influence religion can have over an individual's life if not kept in perspective. Flannery O'Connor addressed the same issues numerous times in her career in books such as *Wise Blood* and *The Violent Bear It Away.* Whether it be in King's Maine, Twain's Mississippi Valley, Faulkner's Mississippi, O'Connor's Deep South, or Nathaniel Hawthorne's Massachussetts, the characters in those stories all reflect the authors' concerns about the human condition, a condition that makes both the authors and their characters brothers and sisters.

However, King does not yet seem to have earned literary recognition. The movie and marketing industries have turned the searchlight away from King's relationship with his country and his literary tradition. It shines instead on the stacks of cash his stories have been able to generate. Because of his money-making potential, King has often been dismissed by critics. Unfortunately, the critics' evaluations have for the most part regarded King's works as insignificant in the literary arena. Is he just a comic-book writer turned novelist? King knows his critics, and he has on several occasions responded to their onslaught:

Almost all of the stuff I have written—and that includes a lot of the funny stuff—was written in a serious frame of mind. I can remember very few occasions when I sat at the typewriter laughing uncontrollably over some wild and crazy bit of fluff I had just finished churning out.... if real—meaning SOMETHING THAT COULD ACTUALLY HAPPEN!!—is your definition of serious, you are in the wrong place and you should by all means leave the building. But please remember as you go that I'm not the only one doing business at this particular site; Franz Kafka had an office here, and George Orwell, and Shirley Jackson, and Jorge Luis Borges, and Jonathan Swift, and Lewis Carroll. A glance at the directory in the lobby shows the present tenants include Thomas Berger, Ray Bradbury, Jonathan Carroll, Thomas Pynchon, Thomas Disch, Kurt Vonnegut, Jr., Peter Straub, Joyce Carol Oates, Isaac Bashevis Singer, Katherine Dunn, and Mark Halpern.... I am doing what I do for the most serious reasons: love, money, and obsession. The tale of the irrational is the sanest way I know of expressing the world in which I live. These tales have served me as instruments of both metaphor and morality; they continue to offer the best window I know on the question of how we perceive things and the corollary question of how we do or do not behave on the basis of our perceptions. I have explored these questions as well as I can within the limits of my talent and intelligence. I am no one's National Book Award or Pulitzer Prize winner, but I'm serious, all right. If you don't believe anything else, believe this: when I take you by your hand and begin to talk, my friend, I believe every word I say. (FPM 607-08)

Just recently, an army of literary critics has been growing in support of King. These are individuals who have taken the time to read books by King and have explored the subtexts. Upon attentiveness to the underlying messages, they cannot understand what is keeping the rest of the intellectual elite in the Dark Ages. Critic Samuel Schuman provides perhaps the most straightforward explanation of why King needs to be taken more seriously: "Anything so popular for so long merits attention, whether it is Stephen King, the Beatles, the Ford Mustang, or Wm. Shakespeare" (107). As I reflected on Schuman's statement, a pattern began to emerge between all of the articles he mentioned; all have at one time or another been labelled popular culture items. Popular culture items have often intimidated intellectuals for some inexplicable reason. Anyone choosing to probe the matter of William Shakespeare will discover that Shakespeare was dismissed by the intellectual elite of his day as popular culture junk. The same can be said about Charles Dickens. Both writers were aiming their material at a wide audience who gave it acceptance. The intellectuals would have little to do with it. Yet, both writers are regarded by today's elite as being two of the giants of English literature. At the time the Beatles emerged on the pop-music scene, adults and intellectuals ran for cover in fear that their traditional music was being overthrown by these young radical hippies. Today, in light of the music presently on the popular culture scene, the Beatles are seen as true artists. The Ford Mustang was not comparable to the Lincoln or the Mercedes-Benz. Today one can see a restored mint Ford Mustang at almost any car show. All of these popular culture items were received with zeal by those outside the elite during the times when they were presented. The pattern emerges: the popular items of one generation become the classic items of the next. History should dictate what Stephen King will be twenty or thirty years from now. Critic Bernard J. Gallagher brings this point to light: "I don't mean to suggest that King is about to replace Shakespeare. I do, however, want to suggest that a cultural phenomenon of such proportions deserves scrutiny" (37). After looking at history, one cannot deny that popular culture carries tremendous implications concerning what will be appreciated in the future.

Those who do appreciate King from an artistic standpoint now are those who are able to make the distinction between what King is doing for popular culture and what the majority of today's artists are doing. While several best-selling authors have relied on formulaic writing for their success, King extends his ties with the American literary tradition by addressing the language and feelings of today through the introduction of freshly conceived plot ideas in each individual work. Says Schuman, "It is noteworthy that King's plots tend to be original with each novel: he does not rewrite the same best-seller over and over again" (114). Except for two or three novels, one cannot find a regurgitation of plot ideas in any King novel. Schuman continues by saying, "So far, at least, King's imagination has been fertile, and he has admirably resisted the temptation to go back to the same lucrative story time after time" (114). This feat in itself is noteworthy. American popular culture today thrives on a regeneration of old ideas; all one needs to do is to look at the ludicrous number of film sequels that stem from an idea formulated years ago—*Halloween, Friday the 13th, Police Academy, Nightmare on Elm Street, Rocky*. It is becoming obvious that the entertainment industry is stopping short of fresh concepts. King never seems to run out of them.

As one should be able to infer by now, King's craft spreads across a wide scope of American artistic contribution. He has managed to build a bridge between popular and classic culture by creating an extension of the American literary tradition he's inherited to the mass-market appeal of the tale of horror. But aside from his apparent success or failure in the bookstores and box offices or an academics' canon, one should simply understand that King is an American in his own unique way. He calls to question what it is to be an American, something he accomplishes by taking a microscope and peering into the diversity of lives that are spread throughout this nation. His song is a cry of the peaks of elation and valleys of sorrow that each and every one of us must encounter at one point or another, and the pride that we take in being of our national blood. The issues beneath the scary and gory manifest of his fiction are an American commentary in disguise. I hope that this journey through Stephen King's fictional realm will leave you with an understanding of the multiplicity of moral, social, and political issues that resonate throughout his canon and their pertinence to our American lives.

Part One:

Stephen King and the Horror Genre

Before exploring Stephen King's America, one should become somewhat familiar with both the Gothic tradition from which King came and the various ideologies that are the foundation of that tradition.

The tale of the unknown has always captured the imagination since the conception of the written word. A survey of literature written during the Middle Ages reveals a catalogue of stories that dealt with the supernatural: *Pearl, Sir Gawain and the Green Knight, The Lais of Marie de France*. All of the stories dealt with powers and forces outside the accepted physical human realm. There is something about the unknown that captures the fancies of the human imagination. Perhaps it is, amidst the suffering that has plagued humankind since its creation, the idea that there is something else capable of harming people that cannot be probed and analyzed.

The tale of popular horror in the twentieth century can find the beginnings of its influence dating back to the early 1800s when England's Mary Wollstonecraft Shelley took on the task with a fellow writer to see who could produce the best ghost story, a task Shelley won after completing *Frankenstein*. In the middle 1800s, Edgar Allen Poe wrote tales of the grotesque to explain his perception of the human condition. Years later, a man named Robert Louis Stevenson locked himself in a room, keeping his family out, and wrote *Dr. Jekyll and Mr. Hyde*. And shortly after that, Bram Stoker wrote *Dracula*. All three stories have had a profound influence on modern tales of the macabre because of their relevance to modern life: an invention that goes awry, the conflict between good and evil in the human heart, a creature of a sexual nature that feeds on human vulnerability.

As the preceding examples illustrate, it is apparent that the interest in the macabre is not a recent fad, although the tale of horror did sink below the mainstream for quite a few years until its resurrection in 1968 with the film *Rosemary's Baby*. The film depicts the seduction of a New York woman by her fellow tenants who are in the service of Satan to find a woman to mother the evil spawn. On the surface, one evaluating the fascination with horror fiction might see it as the demarcation of the human spirit between its moral and immoral impulses. The human spirit is indeed often divided in two—the rational side that wishes to preserve and appreciate life, and the other, darker side that wants nothing more than to destroy it. This conflict is elementary; it can be traced to the initial fall of man in the Garden of Eden. With Adam's and Eve's fall from grace came the predicament to choose between what is good and what is bad for the human condition. In effect, the internal struggle between good and evil basically summarizes humanity, and it is precisely this dilemma that horror fiction addresses. *Dr. Jekyll and Mr. Hyde* is not simply the story of a man's metamorphisis into an evil monster; it is a story that strives to understand the raging influence of evil. In the end, the evil side of Dr. Jekyll becomes so recurrent that he does not even need to drink the potion to induce the change—the change happens spontaneously. *Frankenstein* further supports the foundations of modern horror fiction in its address of the dilemma between a man's humility and his desire to conquer his environment. Dr. Frankenstein's intentions in bringing the dead back to life are ambitious, yet they are plagued with the same curiosity that caused Eve to pluck the fruit from the Tree of Knowledge. The story reinforces the notion that there are some things that humankind was not meant to understand, yet human beings still are not able to grasp this fact. It is because of this awareness of human's ignorance toward their own behavior that the horror writer is perhaps the most humanitarian. The horror writer's monsters are merely the embodiments of the evils that are threaded throughout the human heart.

The reader of horror fiction is able to explore a distorted picture of the world that might be able to offer some explanations of the unexplainable. Because monsters are the conceptions of human evil, the reader is allowed to address his or her own shortcomings and personal fears in a tangible way. Critic Deborah Notkin provides valuable insight concerning the function of horror fiction in describing the human condition by noting that "rather than relaxing in the pleasure of having archetypal fears reduced to the false, the funny and the familiar, our society seems engaged in a desperate search for some sort of horror fantasy at which we cannot laugh" (131). Douglas Winter, author of *Stephen King: The Art of Darkness*, a book which many critics agree belongs in all King readers' libraries, points out:

At a minimum, horror fiction is a means of escape, subliminating the very real and often overpowering horror of everyday life in favor of surreal, exotic, and visionary realms. Escapism is not, of course, necessarily a rewarding experience; indeed, horror fiction's focus upon morbidity and mortality suggests a masochistic or exploitative experience, conjuring subjective fantasies in which our worst fears or darkest desires are brought into tangible existence. (3)

What Winter suggests is that human beings know evil; all they need to do is turn to the media for all the information they need. The function of horror fiction is to allow the reader to see real-life evils become distorted and then sorted out. It also allows the reader to find a safe medium to explore the dark side of his or her own personality and to come out of the experience being grateful that he or she, like the protagonists of the horror novel, has the choice to choose the correct path toward a peaceful, moral existence. The protagonist of a horror story might become an effective mental laboratory guinea pig whose reactions to its tests might aid in the reader's moral advancement. Winter continues by stating, "The confinement of the action to the printed page or motion picture screen renders the irrationality safe, lending our fears the appearance of being controllable" (5). The real world is not a controlled environment; its inhabitants are often helpless to its constant bombardments. The printed page, however, is a controlled environment, one which can be surveyed with scrutiny and used as a valuable teaching tool.

Understanding fear is vital to the development of one's own growth toward maturity, and horror fiction capitalizes on that simple understanding. Fear comes in a a variety of shapes and sizes—fear of rejection, failure, embarrassment, breaking taboos, bodily harm—but, as Stephen King points out, the grandaddy of all fears may well be the one that people most often avoid addressing: death.

We sense the shape [of fear]. Children grasp it easily, forget it, and relearn it as adults. The shape is there, and most of us come to realize what it is sooner or later: it is the shape of a body under a sheet. All our fears add up to one great fear, all our fears are part of that great fear—an arm, a leg, a finger, an ear. We're afraid of the body under the sheet. It's our body. And the great appeal of horror fiction through the ages is that it serves as a rehearsal for our own deaths. (NS 12-13)

The concept that one will someday be reduced to ashes or a rotting body in a coffin is not something that one wants to think about; however, as life progresses, the thought permeates the soul. A child feels primal fears; most often a child's canon of fears consists of fear of the dark, of bodily injury, of monsters. A child is too young to grasp the true concept of death and dying. Adolescents, on the other hand, view the world as full and voluptuous, theirs for the taking. However, as one approaches middle age, the concept of death is not unthinkable. The thought creates anxieties regarding such issues as the degree of one's spirituality and whether one will pay for one's actions in the afterlife. It is when people approach natural death that they are held responsible for their actions on earth, and the thought of atonement for their sins is one that has been repressed by generations of human beings. Indeed one does not even need to turn to horror fiction for explanations of death; all one needs to do is to flip open the copy of the Bible sitting on the front-room table. The book of Revelations has been a recurrent reference for the horror writer, for based on the degree of one's faith, the book of Revelations promises Armegeddon and Judgment Day. This reality proves to be disquieting for any thinking individual. Stephen King's response to this situation is a bit more light-hearted than the average person's feelings about the subject. As a member of the human race who has used what his senses have told him about the human condition, he sees the concept of Armegeddon as a proper way out of this insanity called life:

KING: I think this idea about the end of the world is very liberating. It was for me, and I think most people feel the same way. It's the end of all the shit, and you don't have to be afraid anymore, because the worst has already happened.
Q: That makes horror an escape mechanism to subliminate our primal fear.
KING: I think that's very true. (BB 183)

Perhaps what King says is true; perhaps the human race would be relieved to end the anxieties caused by suffering and the struggle toward salvation. Whatever the consensus concerning death and dying, horror fiction allows the living to explore these issues in a tangible way so that they may evaluate the boundaries of their own mortality.

The text presented so far has suggested that horror fiction addresses the human condition. The human condition is an evolution much like physical growth. One comes out of the womb an infant and then begins a lifelong process that culminates in death. Along the way, one gains experiences that come only with maturity. However, life is more like a wheel than a straight line. One must at various points in his or her life turn back to past years as a reference for moral growth. There are instances experienced as children that provide valuable lessons for later adult life. Adults then pass those lessons on to younger persons so that experience may be transferred and the evolution begins afresh. Horror fiction attempts to point out that it's okay for adults to be afraid of the dark; it's okay to question one's own issue of morality and immorality. Both of these issues are not closed-book cases but rather require a lifetime of effort to formulate plausible solutions. Too often in life do adults try to abandon the lessons learned as children in exchange for a professed adult mentality where to be afraid of the dark is a sign of childish weakness. Horror fiction argues that the growth process does not necessarily lead to moral advancement but rather to the deterioration of morality as one gains a larger exposure to the inherent evil of human beings. Unless one returns to those years of innocence when the sky seemed to have no end, where nature contained endless wonders, when money was just something to buy a soda with, one's existence will be a sorrowful one. One must complete the wheel—to begin as a child, grow old, then turn back to childhood and draw on those experiences and remember them with a sense of education and fondness. Douglas Winter gives perhaps the best summary of the utility of horror fiction in addressing the loop needed to be obtained during mental, moral, and physical growth:

> Our haunted past offers one truth, one answer, that is often obscured by the countless rationalizations, psychological interpretations, and critical insights offered to explain the reading and writing of horror fiction. We knew that truth as children, on those nights when we feared the dark, the slightly open closet door, the certain abyss beneath our bed, yet we were drawn to the darkness and dread. It is a truth that anyone who steps upon a roller coaster must recognize. (SK 23)

A person casually glancing at the content of most horror fiction novels and films will notice that they are riddled with amoral villains, amoral teenagers, rapists, murderers, liars, cheaters, Satanists, and psychopaths. People adverse to horror fiction keep away from it simply because they do not feel the need to expose themselves to the endless carnage that occurs in the tale of horror. These are people who are so tuned in to the horrors of everyday life they have consciously chosen to push the absurdity aside. These are opposites of those who read the horror tales to gain a better understanding of the human condition. Their objections are reasonable. After all, who wants to spend five to ten dollars to jump onto a bandwagon of carnage? Horror fiction does provide plenty of blood and human wreckage. However, if one takes the time to look closely enough at horror fiction, whether it be on the printed page or the screen, one will discover that horror fiction sets its foundations in a traditional Western moral code. This can be applied to even the sleaziest, cheapest carnage thrills such as the *Friday the 13th* film series. This film series is as formulaic as they come. The films typically start out with a camp full of amoral teenagers with nothing but sex on their minds who soon enough are reduced to bloody pulp by the vengeful, hockey-masked Jason Voorhees. A little history on the birth of the evil Voorhees: he is a subhuman creature who is the product of drowning as a young boy while the camp counselors (teenagers) who were supposed to be watching him were engaged in lustful sex. The first episode of the movie saga concerned the slaughtering of teenagers by Jason's mother, who was atoning for her son's death by punishing the amoral. Jason later returns from the dead to continue his mother's vigilant persecution of teenagers after she has her head sliced off with a machete. The victims are always teenagers who are using their time at the camp for smoking pot, getting drunk, and screwing their brains out. With this information, the central thesis should be clear: those who stray from proper morality—meaning abiding to the laws of sound mind and body—are punished. The teenagers who are ruthlessly slaughtered are more often than not engaging in meaningless sex that does not in the most minute way pertain to love. As the films tend to magnify, controlled substances and lustful sex are two of the main vices of the human race. In the tale of horror, those who do not act responsibly are often punished for their actions. As Stephen King points out,

the horror story, beneath its fangs and fright wig, is really as conservative as an Illinois Republican in a three-piece pinstriped suit; that its main purpose is to reaffirm the virtues of the norm by showing us what awful things happen to people who venture into taboo lands. Within the framework of most horror tales we find a moral code so strong it would make a Puritan smile. The horror story most generally not only stands foursquare for the Ten Commandments, it blows them up to tabloid size. (DM 368)

Most people probably do not see horror from this perspective but rather stick to the ideas previously mentioned. What most people see is a re-creation of the most abhorrent of humanity projected onto the screen or written page; most people see nothing to be gained from the horror story but cheap, vulgar thrills.

Aside from the moral code of horror fiction, horror stories also provide reassurance to their audience that they have the choice not to be the atrocities that the stories present. Clive Barker, another prominent author in the field of horror fiction, wrote this about Stephen King's fiction which can be just as easily transferred to any other work in the genre:

King's monsters (human, sub-human, and Cyclopean) may on occasion be comprehensible to us, but they seldom exercise any serious claim on our sympathies. They are moral degenerates, whose colors are plain from the outset. We watch them kick dogs to death, and devour children, and we are reinforced in the questionable certainty that we are not like them; that we are on the side of the angels. (62)

What Barker is suggesting is that horror fiction allows us for once to point a finger and say, "You're the bad guy!" The horror story allows its audience to take comfort in the fact that he or she is not like the antagonist, will never be like the antagonist. Stephen King follows up on Barker's comment with his own insight into the self-promotion horror fiction can supply:

Horror is seen as this barren thing that's supposed to take us over taboo lines, to places where we aren't supposed to be. For a long time people have thought that horror is some kind of radical—a dangerous thing to deal with. But, actually, people who deal in horror…. They're very reactionary. They're agents of the norm. They say, "This is the monster, this is a horrible thing," but at the same time they're saying, "No problem with you. You're cool, because you don't look like this awful thing which has just crawled out of the crater," or whatever. (BB 139-40)

In effect, what both Barker and King are suggesting is that the horror tale allows its audience to take comfort in knowing that he or she is the sane control device in an insane experiment.

Horror fiction is largely allegorical. Aside from its traditional moral implications concerning the individual, it also constructs superficial models as external manifestations of the world that surrounds people in real life. Horror fiction reminds its readers that although they are safe while hidden behind the pages of the novel, the book will eventually be over, and readers will find themselves again back in the physical world. It is one where the unpredictability of its tragedies causes the anxieties that often breed the human and subhuman monsters they'd just read about. While in the book, readers are able to remove themselves from the world around them; when they put it down, they are just as susceptible to evil as the characters contained within it. As Winter brings to light,

horror's truths are judged not by the real fulfillment of its promises, but by the relevance of its fantasies to those of the reader or viewer. Although horror fiction appeals to the source of daydreams—and of nightmares—its context is waking reality. (AOD 4)

Quoting critic Jack Sullivan, Winter continues by stating the paradox created by horror fiction: "What is sought after—the otherwordly—makes us realize how much we need the worldly, but the more we know of the world, the more we need to be rid of it" (4). The horror tale allows the reader to observe a fictional world where reality is distorted in order to give the reader the chance to make presumptions, but the book does indeed end, leaving the reader helpless once again to face a cruel world. All the horror tale can try to achieve is to educate the reader to utilize the accessible observations and apply them to the real world. For example, in Shelley's *Frankenstein*, the protagonist, Dr. Frankenstein, becomes overzealous in his quest for reversing the order of nature. It is a noble goal, but one that carries with it tremendous negative implications. Frankenstein carries out the experiment without reflecting on what the outcome might be; he is only concerned with reaching the end. The reader is presented with the tragedy that results from Frankenstein's carelessness and is left to make his or her own moral deductions about taming in nature what cannot be tamed. Better yet, Frankenstein suggests that living is full of trial and error but that one needs to measure the consequences of one's actions—taking a cliff dive might be exciting, but one does not know if he or she will be plunging straight into a sand bar. One needs first to be able to see far enough ahead to make an assumption of what the end results might be. In the case of *Frankenstein*, the message calls out for attentiveness to anything that is affected by human intervention—natural or technological—whether it be directed at one person or several persons.

The allegorical subtexts of the horror story are the same ones that can be applied to children's fairy tales. Behind each fairy tale adored by children is an underlying message concerning the condition of humanity and collective society. *Hansel and Gretel,* for instance, concerns the treatment of children by adult society. Children, the helpless beings that they are, who are left to fend for themselves too often are likely to be placed in precarious situations. Within the text of King's *The Library Policeman*, a novella in his collection of short novels *Four Past Midnight*, King explains the underlying mechanics of the fairy tale:

"What about Peyton Place? Do you keep a copy of that in the Children's Library just because some of the kids have read it?"

....."No," she said, and he saw that an ill-tempered flush was rising on her cheeks. This was not a woman who was used to having her judgments called into question. "But we do keep stories about house-breaking, parental abuse, and burglary. I am speaking, of course, of 'Goldilocks and the Three Bears,' 'Hansel and Gretel,' and 'Jack and the Beanstalk.'" (432)

The same subtexts that apply to the stories King mentions in this passage can be applied to horror fiction. Douglas Winter, quoting D.H. Lawrence writing about Edgar Allen Poe's horror fiction, writes that "it is lurid and melodramatic, but it is true" (AOD 3-4). To further support the notion of allegory in horror fiction and specifically Stephen King's fiction, Samuel Schuman argues that:

the "pleasing allegorical feel" about which King speaks is a peculiar kind of psychological allegory, for the readings between the lines to which King invites us invariably discuss the political, social, and economic anxieties of the contemporary individual. For example, *Carrie*, according to King, is actually a feminist novel which confronts a young woman's psychic conflict when she attempts to live as a strong and autonomous individual in a culture that would prefer to see her as a passive and powerless piece of femininity. (38)

Carrie is about an adolescent girl who is subjected to both the ridicule of her classmates because of both her awkward appearance and timid personality, and the religious fanaticism of her fundamentalist mother. Later in the novel, when Carrie tries to achieve her femininity by dressing up for her high school prom, she is doused in pig blood by her adolescent tormentors. When she returns home after wreaking havoc on those who shamed her, she walks right in to the second trap: her mother's accusations. Carrie cannot assert an autonomous identity as a female, an externally unattractive female. When she tries to break out of her shell, both her peers and her mother try to put her back in. The novel is the story of a Cinderella-gone-bad; there is no Prince Charming to come back to fit the glass slipper onto her foot and take her away from a life of suppression. Death and destruction are the end results as an antagonistic society takes away the only thing Carrie has: the chance to love herself.

The following item was obtained from the Special Collections Department of the Raymond H. Fogler Library at the University of Maine at Orono. It is an excerpt from a piece of fan mail written to Stephen King by a young male adolescent concerning the novel *Carrie*:

What really got me was that I knew a girl that went to my school that was like Carrie only. Her name is Ramona Benkins. Her name was bad enough. Carrie was good looking under everything. But Ramona was just ugly. Her mother told her that boys were evil and no good so she was parinoid [sic] about boys and wouldent [sic] let one come near her. Which made all the boys chase her and make her cry. I regret to say I did it too. I dident [sic] think nothing of it untill [sic] I read your book and saw how Ramona must have felt. I don't know how I could have been such an asshole[.] I'm trying to get her number so I can call and apologize. So thank you very much for you book[.] It made me a little more mature.

P.S. You can tell I'm not a brains from my letter[.]
I'm sorta a Billy Nolan [the dimwit boyfriend of Carrie's primary tormentor, Chris Hargenson].

This letter more than suggests that the subtexts of the horror novel *Carrie* affected this young boy in a way applicable to his waking life. It was able to make him look at himself and then at the world around him, which is full of insecure persecutors much like those both in the novel itself and the school that he attended. The preceding excerpt is an example that shows that even a young person can draw connections between the real and unreal to make meaningful evaluations about the human condition. In support of King's significance when writing horror, in the February 7, 1978, issue of *The Maine Times*, newswriter David Chute, in his review of King's collection of short stories *Night Shift* [the review also obtained from the Fogler Library], states that

what King is doing may not be great art, but it has something in common with art. Is it possible that people find his work disturbing...because it gets to them on a level they don't expect of entertainment, precisely, in other words, because it begins with something real and develops it in imagination, almost like a work of art? (4)

Burton Hatlen, a professor of English at UMO who once taught King as a student, follows up on the effectiveness of horror fiction in drawing a connection between fiction and reality for the reader in this speculation about Shirley Jackson: "the power of *The Haunting of Hill House*, like the power of Poe's stories, arises directly from this blurring of the line that separates the 'objective' from the 'subjective,' the 'real' from the 'imaginary' " (89). Horror fiction blends the real and the unreal to produce a whole experience that allows the reader to utilize the imaginary for application to reality through horror's allegorical mechanisms.

As has been said, horror fiction serves two vital yet sometimes opposing functions of allegory and ambiguity which makes the lines separating reality and unreality less conspicuous. Stephen King has taken advantage of these utilities and sculpted them to pertain to modern times—a book like *The Shining*, for instance, is both allegorical in its superficial construct of a consuming capitalist economy (the Overlook Hotel) and ambiguous in its portrayal of reality (the ghosts that talk to Jack Torrance inside of the hotel).

Although there are several authors both living and deceased who have earned reputations as being masters of the macabre, one cannot deny that King has catapulted the genre into realms unthought of before his books hit the stands. Nearly 80 million copies of King's books have sold worldwide, making him the most successful author of horror fiction in the history of English literature. No one has come close to the popularity he has achieved. There are a number of reasons for this.

First, he loves the English language and has taken it upon himself to carry out the tradition of his Gothic literary predecessors. His own canon gives a good indication of the amount of reading in the genre he has accomplished.

Second, he has a firm understanding of the principles of horror fiction.

Third, he has perhaps the most active imagination among popular fiction writers today.

Fourth, he does not try to bog down his readers with overdeveloped, complex plots and language. He writes about common Americans with whom his readers can identify. He puts his characters in situations that his readers can sympathize with. When he writes about them, it does not matter what age, sex, race or region of America he is discussing; when he writes, he seems to possess an uncanny ability to capture the images and dialogues of whomever he is writing about, whether it be a Texas service station man or a high-ranking Republican government official. He talks to his readers and he understands their feelings, and he is able to transfer those familiarities into tales of horror in the Gothic tradition. But most important of King's qualities as a writer, aside from his value as an entertainer, is that he may be the most significant spokesperson of contemporary America among popular culture artists today, a skill that has been accumulated over years of concern with artistic expression.

King's roots as a writer go back to early childhood. In his book *The Unseen King*, author Tyson Blue explains that King had already begun writing tales of the unnatural when he was barely a teenager. King himself admits that he was fascinated with horror stories and films when he was a young child. Anyone reading a King book can see clearly that he knows about literature of all genres including the horror genre. Burton Hatlen explains in an interview later in this book that King was highly influenced by writers such as Shirley Jackson, William Faulkner, John Steinbeck, and William Carlos Williams. King often pulls quotes from his favorite works to tie in with the tale he is unraveling. Hatlen also points out that during his college years, King read an average of a book a day. Someone that dedicated can hardly be ignorant of the thoughts and issues significant to American literature and culture. King has merely continued the functions of earlier significant writers and spread them to a wider audience. As critic Ben Indick explains,

excess is only one element King inherited from the Gothicists. There is another, far more important. For Stephen King, who remembers shuddering through monster films as a child and claims he still cannot sleep without at least one light glowing in the house, the indispensable mainspring in his stories is Fear. Its origins may be psychological, physical, or even supernatural, but the fear itself is real, and his horror stories succeed because his readers share it.... Walpole's school had foundered when fear lost its rationality. Drs. Van Helsing and Freud rediscovered it beneath Prince Albert coats. King has put it into the shopping basket, next to the tomato sauce, the Sanka and the Tab. Fear has become a commonplace, no longer the evil dispensation of noble or supernatural villains. No one can be trusted, not teenaged school kids, not a cop or a prosaic motel-keeper, not even a small baby. It is a world with neither security nor stability. (166-67)

In his fiction, King often illustrates the issues that have impact on American society today much in the same way that his literary predecessors addressed the issues facing them when they were writing. King, like the Gothic traditionalists, goes one step further by adding elements of fear, which, regardless of who or where King is writing about, are universal and establish a common ground for all of his readers. As Indick points out, "In his own distinctive style are mirrored the major traditions he has inherited" (153). People like King's books because within them the personal lives of the characters are disclosed, yet the readers are also treated to scenes of fear to which they can personally relate, a combination of content that has achieved King's literary predecessors their greatness.

While there are many authors today who can profess to be social or political writers—E.L Doctorow (*The Book of Daniel*), Tom Clancy (*The Hunt for Red October* and *Clear and Present Danger*), and Scott Turow (*Presumed Innocent* and *The Burden of Proof*)—there are few writers who have covered the broad landscapes of America utilizing inherited literary traditions, especially the Gothic, the way King has in the modern popular culture scene. His books involve life in both big cities and small towns; King's small towns create settings that King believes are the multiple epicenters of the human spirit in America. Within the frameworks of each individual small town are social and personal networks that resemble in and of themselves one giant organism in their ability to combine each individual component into one breathing whole because of the lack of separation and isolation that can result from living in a big city. By using these settings, King creates an effective foundation for social commentary. King also explores the broad range of social problems that face Americans daily—the question of moral choice, technology, religion, government, capitalism, the repression that can result from social organization of any form—and he knows of no better way to discuss these issues than the horror tale, which effectively masks the true issues at hand lying beneath, something he explains in his Foreword to *Night Shift*:

When you read horror, you don't really believe what you read. You don't believe in vampires, werewolves, trucks that suddenly start up and drive themselves. The horrors that we all do believe in are the sort that Dostoyevsky and Albee and MacDonald write about: hate, alienation, growing lovelessly old, tottering out into a hostile world on the unsteady legs of adolescence. (NS 4)

Author Chelsea Quinn Yarbro follows up on King's usage of the horror story to create social allegory in her summary of *The Shining*. The novel is about a man and his family who move into a hotel to maintain it during the winter season. While in the hotel, the Overlook, ghosts of the hotel's haunted past pull protagonist Jack Torrance into their lair and complete the seduction by turning Torrance against his family. What appears to be a haunted house story is really much, much, more: it is about the disintegration of a family due to a man's internal struggle brought on by the expectations of a patriarchal society that preaches the importance of success in both his chosen trade and in his role as provider. When father Jack bows to his vices and listens to the ghosts of the past, there is still a glimmer of hope in that he can find redemption in bonding with his family, one of the small circles of love that necessitate survival in King's fiction. However, Jack is unable to form that bond, and the destruction of the man ensues. Says Yarbro:

King's skill in story-telling disguises this so that the reader is more caught up in the victimization of the family than in the manipulations of the mind that are the source of the trouble. In this context it is not important whether the things Jack sees are actual or invented or past events in the hotel's history. Jack's state of mind calls these demons forth, just as the fate of his son Danny is to be the blessed spirit or pure soul that sees the fall from grace and all that it entails and can do little or nothing to prevent or change the destruction taking place, within the house and within his father. (49)

One can infer from Yarbro's explanation that in *The Shining*, King is up to his usual business. He has covered up the sources of all the world's problems—human beings—with the superficial outer shells of misfortune and supernatural interference. If one reads the novel more closely between the lines, one will discover that much of the hotel's past is stained with moral and political corruption, capitalist style. Hatlen follows Yarbro's observations by writing that:

generically, *The Shining* is a haunted-house story. King based his immediately preceding novel, *Salem's Lot*, on a classic horror story, Bram Stoker's *Dracula*; and *The Shining* also seems to have been born out of an impluse to lay claim to the classic tradition of horror fiction. Specifically, *The Shining* borrows from and pays homage to certain tales of Poe and Shirley Jackson's *The Haunting of Hill House*.... In particular, King follows both Poe and Jackson in seeing the haunted house as a metaphor for or a manifestation of a disordered human mind. (88)

Like other horror stories that have masked social commentary behind the grotesque (*Friday the 13th*), King's stories use supernatural forces and subhuman creatures to hide the messages beneath. While many may argue that those making the *Friday the 13th* series were not aware of the moral questions the films were raising but rather were out to make a buck, one who has read a good sample of King's fiction cannot deny them. As critic Bernard J. Gallagher explains,

the insight which King offers into the work of horror is based upon a bimodal or dualistic vision which insists upon the necessity of reading between the lines. The first mode or level which King describes is the "gross out" level—i.e. that level at which a cultural norm is violated for shock effect.... The second and subtextual level—the between the lines, so to speak—he describes is the artistic level, that is, a second level at which horror novels seek to probe "phobic pressure points" which address archetypal, "political, economic, and psychological rather than supernatural fears." (38)

It has already been stated that King is a significant commentator of the human condition in America in light of his success as an entertainer. What remains to be seen are the fine points of King's subtexts and the powerful utilization of horror fiction that supports them. No one really needs to be told of King's power to frighten, and the purpose of the next section is not to interview King's villains and archvillains but to point out to those who have not yet been able to read between King's lines the plethora of issues that need nothing but an extra lamp to be flicked on so that one may see them. Once the reader is able to read into the subtexts of Stephen King's fiction, he or she will come out of one of his books with much more than a good scare.

Part Two:

Stephen King's America

Beneath their archetypal trappings, King's novels evoke the troubled atmosphere of contemporary America, one harried as much by the realities of corrupt government, technology run rampant, and an uncertain domestic life as by monsters and ghosts and other mythical products of the human imagination.

Tom Newhouse
The Gothic World of Stephen King

Traversing King's American Terrain

Those writers who have achieved greatness in American literature have often built the foundations of their prose in writing about specific regions of America. Writers such as Mark Twain, William Faulkner, and Flannery O'Connor were able to to examine the human condition most effectively when describing the regions most familiar to them. Stephen King, like his literary predecessors, has also claimed an American region of his own—Maine, an area of the country of which King is an intimate part—as a setting for his exploration of humanity. This tendency of authors to adopt a region from which to probe humanity becomes significant when observed collectively; if one were to strip away the geography and dialect of any piece of regional literature, one would soon discover that underneath those regional manifestations are universal concerns and issues about humanity that unite all distinctive regional fictions together.

While King has followed the footsteps of his literary predecessors in utilizing a specific area of America as an epicenter from which his portrayal of American life spreads out, he has gone one step further by daring to venture outward from those surroundings that are most familiar to him. He has on several occasions shifted away from Maine and travelled across the wide expanse of the country to relocate the setting for his fiction: Junction City, Iowa (*The Library Policeman*), Colorado (*The Shining* and *Misery*), Pittsburgh, Pennsylvania (*Christine*), New York and Virginia (*Firestarter*), and finally, a journey west that begins in the extreme East (*The Stand* and *The Talisman*). This confidence to move outside of his familiar region may be accredited to King's firm understanding of the universality of the human condition, that regardless of the time or place, the trials and situations facing humanity are uniform.

What makes King such a vital contributor to American literature is that he has combined a wholeness of vision with a thorough education in past significant fictions concerned with American life—fictions best exemplified in works by Twain, Faulkner, O'Connor, and John Steinbeck. He has been able to expand on the American

31

literary tradition by abiding by its precepts; at the same time, he has been able to make fiction fun for modern audiences. As mentioned, he has chosen a particular region from which to write about, much like his literary predecessors, yet he has been able to move elsewhere. But, most important, he, like his predecessors, has been able to comment on the human condition in America, a commentary that is hidden beneath the manifestations of the text.

Even before readers make the effort to grasp the subtextual references to American humanity in an American novel, they can make several generalizations readily apparent when summarizing life in America. For instance, Americans have for two centuries prided themselves on being living parts of the land of the free. They have the right to free speech, the right to choose religion, the right to trial by jury of peers, and rights to happiness and liberty. They have the power to choose who will lead their country. They have access to an unending supply of food. They have the motivation to better themselves in a free market economy that could reward them with material wealth. Seen from this light there is not much that can be said against the world's greatest superpower. Yet while Americans pride themselves on living in the planet's greatest country, they are still human beings with the same shortcomings as any other individuals regardless of nationality. While America boasts its superiority, it leads the world in crime. It has a high rate of substance abuse. Women are raped and beaten by men and then shamed in court by a male-dominated criminal justice system. There are millions of homeless, millions of unemployed. America has corrupt politicians who are willing to sell the principles they swore to uphold in order to obtain a spot on organized crime's payroll. The country has seen a widespread epidemic in AIDS that has killed thousands. One can be blinded with textbook descriptions of an American dream, but deep inside one also knows that America is a difficult place to live despite its freedoms. Like stripping away the manifestations of a text in order to see its subtexts, so can the multiple facets of nationalities be removed to reveal that beneath varying skin colors and languages is one human heart with common emotions and concerns, an aspect that renders Americans like foreigners. It is this recognition of one universal human heart that is the foundation of Stephen King's fiction.

A brief history of events in King's life may prove to reveal his fault with America despite its promises of fruitful life. He was raised by a fundamentalist Methodist mother in an adamantly Republican Maine, both of which began to shape his thoughts and feelings before he was old enough to formulate them for himself. Later in his life, he rebuked both of them. In college, he became politically active, participating in seminars and protests. When marching for peace during the Vietnam war, he was struck by a fraternity boy who thought of King as a long-haired radical. Soon after he completed his bachelor's degree at the University of Maine at Orono, he was arrested by a policeman who claimed King was staggeringly drunk and apprehended him for public intoxication. In court, the verdict was not guilty. The concern at the time was that King had been arrested merely because of his appearance—his shaggy long hair triggering the word "hippie" among his conservative peers. He had been bombarded by the media after the massacre at Kent State University where several students were shot down by law enforcement representatives during a peace demonstration. Later in his life, still faithful to the Republican party, King found his political views in disarray with the disclosure of the Watergate scandal. He has since been a supporter of the Democratic party and has seen his political favorites defeated by their conservative counterparts who many believe have managed to spiral the country into a national debt it will never get out of.

More than the subjective events in King's life appear to have caused him to scrutinize American society in his writing. His writing also indicates a desire to understand the human condition as it exists in the world, specifically in the country, he inhabits. There also seems to be a plethora of other issues bearing down on America that riddle his intellect: the motivating factors that cause people to violently turn against one another; the human spirit's tendency to rebel; the drive toward material wealth created by America's economic system that causes men and women to alienate themselves from loved ones in search of another buck; a government that is elected popularly by a body of constituents who turn their undying faith over to it only to have it bite the hands that fed it. However, although the list is long, King's main preoccupation seems to be with the simple struggle between good and evil, right and wrong, that wages itself in human beings daily.

It is the combination of an unbreachable desire to probe the country he lives in and a love for life amidst pain and suffering that has motivated King to write. His public, well aware of the countless adversities facing them in contemporary society, may find a meaningful prophet in the master of the modern horror novel.

Critic Bernadette Lynn Bosky points out in her essay "The Mind's a Monkey: Character and Psychology in Stephen King's

Recent Fiction" that "one reason for Stephen King's overwhelming popularity as a writer is that the magic mirror of his fiction shows us an image of ourselves and our world that we want to believe—at least for as long as we join him in his books" (237). King's novels offer his readers sanctuary in that they give an accurate portrayal of the degree of suffering in one's lifetime, yet they offer the hope of moral redemption and salvation; in his books, people have free will to choose their destinies. Their destinies are often centered around their moral choices. In an America where happy endings are rare, his novels allow people to enter a cruel world and for once see people who have the power to overcome the evil staring down at them. Bosky adds to her argument that

King's overall approach to character, vital to both his fantastic fiction and his occasional non-fantastic works, is based in credible psychologizing that also reaffirms notions his readers believe or would like to believe: the importance of choice, the existence of the supernatural, the power of love. He presents a romantic but not simplistic view of the mind, which includes the values of both irrational and logical reaction, although it points out the limitations of each. As King's characters make their choices and try to maintain the delicate balance of mind the human condition calls for, the reader feels affection for them and gains understanding of them. (236)

King's novels provide an appropriate emotional outlet for Americans in that they portray characters who believe themselves to be larger than life but who find in the end they are all swimming in the same cesspool of human vulnerability. They reflect the issues and concerns of contemporary America—moral choice and the search for the self, the rites of passage and the end of innocence, fear of a technology that is growing faster than it can be understood, a self-serving government that hides its vices, the loss of self in the shadow of capitalist principles, the fear of the loss of individuality under the clamps of social organization, the need for intimate love and friendships to share in happiness and in suffering—and they address them in a context that allows readers to be entertained as well as be taught a course in exploring themselves and the America they live in.

King's novels are also effective in their thorough exploration of the varying regions and people of America. As has already been mentioned, while he does place the bulk of his fiction in his native Maine, he at times leaves his state to probe other spots on the map. Even when he writes about Maine, the fictional and non-fictional locations he uses are almost always small towns, and the motivation behind this appears to be that the small towns represented could be any small town in America. While the bulk of big news takes place in metropolitan cities, what King tries to point out is that the true heart of America lies in the small towns that are the flea-specks on state maps; the small towns that in their own eccentric way form microcosms separate from the hustle and bustle of the country's industrial centers. It is within his portrayal of small-town life that King is most effective in his comment on the human condition for it reduces the degree of diversity between neighbors, allowing King to make a more convincing argument about the commonness of human nature. Outside of the individual regions and towns of the country, King does not concern himself with solely one class of individuals. He is just as concerned about the trials and tribulations of the employee working the night shift at a rundown textile mill as he is about a man running for the Senate. Each and every American appeals to Stephen King, and his canon provides an accurate barometer of the individual characteristics that make each American unique. At the same time he realizes that Americans form a wide array of personalities, he is aware they are all one in their shared concerns about humanity—an understanding that makes King, in his own special way, unique.

A closer surveillance of the multiple issues pertinent to American life that are threaded throughout King's fiction should prove that there is a substance in his stories that dips much deeper than the monsters and villains easily recognized on the surface. With this recognition should come an awareness that King has indeed establshed a canon of fiction that becomes a significant extension of both twentieth-century American literature and the essential need to understand and interpret the American human condition.

I. The Struggle for Personal Morality in America

In the majority of his fiction, Stephen King seems to understand that while the world is broken up into societies and cultures for the sake of organization, individual people themselves are the driving forces behind change. An analytical interpretation of the human condition in King's fiction must begin with and focus on the individuals that join together to form larger collective bodies. After all, at the center of each and every issue facing people today is a question of moral choice: is it right to dump chemical wastes into streams and lakes? Is it right to abort an unborn child, and, if so, is it or is it not murder? Is it right to let one's sixteen-year-old daughter go on a weekend ski-trip with her boyfriend? Should one slip a candy bar in his pocket if no one is looking? The list of choices that call morality into play are endless. All of these questions have been subjectively called into debate in each and every American's mind, and they all center around the simple differentiation between right and wrong. While evil is a mainstay in the human heart, the magic of the human condition rests in its capacity to do good in spite of the adversities that prompt evil action. At the center of all things that result from human interference is the need to question what is right and what is wrong. It is the answers to these questions that have the largest impact on the human condition.

The appeal of King's fiction to his readers rests in the fact that it constantly raises the question of morality; it recognizes the pervasiveness of evil, but it also aims to prove that the forces of good, when formed behind a collaboration of human hearts to enforce good, will almost always reign over evil. It is only when the protagonists of King's stories alienate themselves from fellow human beings in their battles against evil while failing to recognize their own human flaws that they fall—a notion that reinforces the idea of strength in numbers, that the emphasis in a peaceful human condition is grounded in the collective will to do good. In other words, progress begins with the individual, but there must be a union of good will in order for the human race to further itself. This romantic notion of the potential good residing in the human heart is

36

something that critic Deborah Notkin believes gives King his popular draw:

Stephen King has achieved unprecedented popularity as a writer of horror fiction, largely because he understands the attraction of fantastic horror to the denizen of the late 20th century, and because, paradoxical though it may sound, he has reassurance to bring us. For whether he is writing about vampires, about the death of 99 percent of the population, or about innocent little girls with the power to break the earth in half, King never stops emphasizing his essential liking for people. He does not, of course, paint a rosy picture of a loving and flawless human race; he simply focuses, again and again, on people doing the right things in difficult situations, on people who behave slightly better than we expect. The overwhelming impression to be gained from reading King's books is that the kinks and the sadists are the exception, not the rule. In these novels, the average person is reasonably honest, caring and upright, and can be relied upon in most circumstances—not a fashionable concept, these days, but one which has obvious attractions for contemporary audiences. (232)

King's power in his fiction is an adamant belief in a personal moral code; those who behave morally and make correct moral choices when faced with adversities are those who are likely to win the fight against evil. Those characters in King's fiction who do not behave morally and rather surrender the well-being of others for evil or selfish motives are those who are ultimately destroyed. *Needful Things* is a prime reference of his idealized moral code. In the novel, entrepreneur Leland Gaunt opens shop in the town of Castle Rock. The name of his shop, Needful Things, is a primary indication of what is stored inside; his inventory consists of those material objects that each resident of Castle Rock most desires. As Gaunt predicts, Castle Rock's residents are willing to pay almost any price for their fancies. Gaunt's price includes two parts—a sum of money, and, most importantly, a trick to be played on a person of his selection. Each and every patron who steps through the door of Needful Things is faced with a moral choice: should they refuse access to the objects they desperately want and deny the risk of injuring their peers, or should they jump at the offer, abandoning any notion of brotherhood for the sake of personal gain? Unfortunately, most choose the latter, augmenting the mistrust among neighbors that had already been breeding prior to Gaunt's grand opening. Castle Rock's agreement to allow Gaunt, who capitalizes on their selfishness to corrupt it, turns neighbor against neighbor until widespread violence reduces the town to ashes. Two Castle Rockians, Polly Chalmers and Sheriff Alan Pangborn, who are engaged in a love affair, are also seduced by Gaunt's 'needful things,' but, after agonizing deliberation, reject his prizes and acknowledge his seductive scheme; their love for each other shines through the dark veil of their selfishness, and they join together against Gaunt. Likewise, Deputy Norris Ridgewick, although having played a major part in Gaunt's grand plan after performing a trick that triggers murder, also atones for his mistake by rushing to the rescue of Alan and Polly when Gaunt confronts them. In the end, Polly, Alan, and Norris are able to survive simply because they value human bonding over selfish motives. As Notkin's passage suggests, the concept of consequences arising from moral choice such as those portrayed in *Needful Things* is far from fresh or imaginative, but it is one that never loses its flavor or appeal with contemporary audiences. Inside the heart of us is a desire to see the selfishly wicked punished; this conviction is adequately exemplified in the real-life case of convicted serial killer Ted Bundy, who raped and tortured dozens of young girls from Florida to Washington. At his execution, when the switch was thrown, an audience standing outside cheered; he who acted selfishly and immorally against his fellow sisters was served his just desserts.

Yet another aspect of King's fiction pertinent to morality and the human condition is that his monsters and villians stem directly from human evil. His readers like to see his antagonists destroyed because they represent the human monsters that live among the real world— Rev. Jim Jones, Richard Speck, Charles Manson, John Wayne Gacy, Richard Ramirez, Jeffrey Dahmer: these are the extreme atrocities and perversions of the human spirit, the extreme examples of the breach in morality that threatens humankind. Burton Hatlen points out that:

while King recognizes that serial killers truly do exist, he suggests that our fascination with them moves them into the same mythic territory where vampires live; and the myths we create about such people tell us as much about ourselves as they do about the psychopathology of sex murderers. Vampires, killer cars, and rubber-coated sex murderers—all crawl out of the "myth-pool in which we all bathe communally".... We, not King, have created these creatures; and he gives them back to us, to tell us something about ourselves. (84)

It may be that society's tendency to glamorize or raise to cult status psychopaths arises from a need to use those evil-doers as barometrical instruments measuring the sanity and morality of those who condemn their actions. An equally effective measuring device, King's fiction often allows readers to point fingers at the villains contained within and to cherish the truth or contemplate the untruth of each individual's morality.

As mentioned, King's fiction serves to argue that society needs a collective good will. However, that collective good will obviously starts at the individual level. While human beings make haste in accusing others of immoral actions, they often ignore consideration of how to obtain their own moral maturity—a paradox that reveals itself often in King's canon. Each one of King's novels portrays a protagonist or group of protagonists who must make moral decisions that will have impact on their fates. Without moral maturity, both people and King's characters suffer from their inability to heed the consequences of moral differentiation, therefore increasing the difficulty to act on behalf of goodness. Bernadette Lynn Bosky, making reference to one of King's most descript portrayals of moral choice, *Pet Sematary*, summarizes this concern of King's when she points out that:

King realistically presents his characters with the choice of which interior voice to follow and which to silence. The tragedy of *Pet Sematary* is that Louis Creed begins to follow his intuitions only when he should begin to doubt them. His premonition regarding Gage and his visitation from Pascow are dismissed because they do not fit into his materialistic worldview. (231)

Without an individual's ability to make correct moral decisions, adverse conditions often become unavoidable. As Bosky brings to light, the fate of Louis Creed in *Pet Sematary* results from his anger with life for taking away his only son, Gage, who was struck by a semi-trailer truck when trying to cross a busy highway. Creed's reaction to his son's death is to exhume the corpse and bury it an ancient Indian burial ground behind the pet cemetery near his home, a ground that was once sacred to a tribe of Micmac Indians. Creed had already used the sacred ground to bury his cat, Churchill, when it was struck by a truck. The cat had come back from the dead, but was not the same cat: its spirit had been removed by the death process. What Louis saw in the resurrected Churchill was not the fluffy cat his daughter, Ellie, was fond of but rather an evil reincarnation. Rather than reviewing the results of the cat's return from the burial site and applying that knowledge to the horrible potential it could have with a human being, Louis ignores his wiser intuition not to play with death but rather confronts fate. What returns from the burial ground is a soiled, evil, blood-thirsty version of his son. Critic Samuel Schuman supports Bosky's observation when he suggests that:

it should be clear...that the thematic center of the novel derives from the clear moral judgment that it is sinful for humans to tamper with mortality. Creed falls, through love, into a sin the mirror opposite of murder: he does not make the living into the dead; he tries to make the dead to live again, and in so doing brings down upon himself and his family a progressive nightmare from which there is no escape. Within a plot of considerable imaginative ambition, King embeds a thematic core which would be gratifying to the most ardent fundamentalist. (113)

It is Creed's inability to make the distinction between the right and wrong courses of action that creates the fall of his subjective world. His fall is correlative with that of Victor Frankenstein—his failure to make the correct moral choice when pursuing a selfish goal brings destruction and sorrow to both him and his family.

Yet another example of a King character who suffers from a lapse in correct moral choice is Harold Lauder, one of the survivors of the flu epidemic in *The Stand*. Harold is a young social outcast much like the characters that find places in almost every King story. Harold is overweight, unattractive, and unable to communicate with other human beings intimately. When he falls in love with Frannie Goldsmith, his older sister's friend who also survived the epidemic, he cannot outwardly tell her of his feelings but rather keeps them trapped in a personal diary. When Frannie falls in love with Stu Redman, Harold's reaction is not to accept defeat but to allow his bitterness against both of them to mount. Frannie, Stu, and the rest of the Free Zone Committee (the representatives of the army of good will established in the post-epidemic world) all try to make Harold a welcome member, but he rejects them. He cannot accept the fact that he is living in a new world, one needing reconstruction because of the massive population reduction from the superflu, and that the new world will give him an opportunity to become something that he never was in his previous life: a working cog in the mechanism of a meaningful society. As Bosky points out, "Harold will not let himself realize that his rejection of hope and change also murders his new, better self before it is born" (229). Harold is put in a position to accept the bond his Free Zone friends offer him or to reject it for the fulfillment of the destruction of the society he resented previously.

His choice to reject human bonding in favor of the selfish goals offered by Randall Flagg, the adversary of the Free Zone, leads to Harold's downfall. Bosky supports this when she observes that:

[one of the] most stunning scenes of "the free will to do evil or deny it" in King's fiction [has] little or nothing to do with the supernatural. Harold Lauder's acceptance of all-consuming hatred in *The Stand*...show[s] that no matter how much or little control we have over situations, we always choose whether or not to control our emotional reactions to these situations. (227)

Both Louis Creed and Harold Lauder may be seen as manifestations of real-life moral issues relevant to modern America. Creed's desire to interfere with the natural death process is applicable to the modern-day concerns about death control—euthanasia—while Harold Lauder's refusal to relinquish his rage over past wrongs can be applied to the continuous warring between countries on the national level and individuals on the domestic level. Both Louis and Harold serve to explicate King's interpretation of what happens when people fail to make correct moral decisions.

When readers are evaluating evil in King's books, they must be able to identify both the outright manifestations of evil and the sources of their power. No one can deny that characters like Randall Flagg, Barlow ('Salem's Lot*), Pennywise the Clown (*It*), Morgan Sloat (*The Talisman*), and George Stark (*The Dark Half*) are purely concentrated evil; readers can reasonably dismiss any notion of moral redemption for these villains. These evil incarnations serve no other purpose than to destroy humanity and cloud their victims' moral discretion with their dark influences. The dark forces in King's fiction almost always derive their power from the weakness and vulnerabilities of their prey; were it not for human imperfections, these entities would not exert the degree of influence that they are able to carry out. In his book *Stephen King, The Second Decade: Danse Macabre to The Dark Half*, written for the Twayne United States Authors Series, Tony Magistrale argues that

like the Overlook Hotel, the Tommyknockers, Christine, It, and other examples of maleficence in King's world, evil requires some element of human weakness—ignorance, avarice, anger, rejection, indifference, jealousy—as a means for the initial corruption of innocence. (244)

Burton Hatlen follows up on this when he suggests that "I am here proposing that King sees both Good and Evil as primarily subjective and intersubjective phenomena" (88). In other words, Hatlen is assuming that evil in King's fiction is not a sovereign body separate from humanity but rather is often the product of the accumulated negative impulses inside people, the same people who create their own monsters through their inabilities to love each other and act morally.

The tragedies in King's fiction lie not so much in the victims of evil manifestations but in the stories' central characters' tendency to bow to their human shortcomings, allowing evil to flourish. A majority of King's books place the central protagonists in positions to follow their moral or immoral impulses. Those who consider the implications of acting immorally and act accordingly are those who overcome evil; those who succumb to the immediate gratification that evil offers are those who eventually fall. Take the case of Arnie Cunningham in *Christine*. Arnie is another Harold-Lauder-type character who is rejected by his peers because of his peculiarity and unattractive looks. When he finds Christine, a '57 Plymouth Fury, he finds a new identity. He is able to stand up to his tormentors. He starts dating the most beautiful girl in his high school. The car, a symbol of identity in a young person's life, brings Arnie a sense of confidence. Yet while Christine has rewarded him with a fresh identity, she has also turned him into a hostile, self-serving individual. She kills all of those who have done or intend to do Arnie wrong; she brings his evil impulses to a horrifying reality. At first, Arnie is ignorant of Christine's malicious actions. But as the story continues, and Arnie becomes vaguely aware that since Christine has been in his life, people have been suffering, he must decide whether to scrap her, which would save lives and return Arnie to the thoughtful, caring boy he used to be, or to keep her and the self-fulfilling promises she offers him. Arnie makes his decision in the following scene:

In fact, there were times when he didn't want the car at all. There were times when he felt he would be better off just...well, junking it. Not that he ever would, or could. It was just that, sometimes (in the sweaty, shaking aftermath of that dream last night, for instance), he felt that if he got rid of it, he would be...happier..."Don't worry," Arnie whispered. He ran his hand slowly over the dashboard, loving the feel of it. Yes, the car frightened him sometimes. And he supposed his father was right; it had changed his life to some degree. But he could no more junk it than he could commit suicide. (264)

Arnie is in a position to make a moral choice: trash the car and save both others and himself from her evil, or keep her and continue to feed on the gratifications she can give him. His choice to keep her results in the deaths of several others and ultimately himself.

In another example where moral choice is called to question in King's fiction, Pop Merrill, the pawn shop owner in *The Sun Dog*, a novella in *Four Past Midnight*, has possession of a young boy's Polaroid Sun 660 camera that has caused some unrest due to the recurring picture it takes. Regardless of the person or object the camera is aimed at, the camera continuously produces an image of an angry dog. When Pop and Kevin Delevan, the camera's owner, put the pictures together in succession, it becomes apparent that the dog is turning and moving closer to the front of the picture, looking as though it is preparing to strike. Each successive snapshot brings it nearer until there is no doubt that the dog means to escape and exercise its rage. After becoming aware of the camera's oddity, Pop, a true capitalist, is drawn to its queerness and covets it with the intent of making a profit despite comprehending the implications of potential disaster accompanying it. At one particular point, as the possiblity of the dog's intentions becomes more real to Pop, Pop begins to realize that maybe he could do the world and himself a favor by destroying the camera.

Why not get rid of the camera right here? he thought suddenly. You can. Just get out, walk to the guardrail there, and toss her over. All gone. Goodbye.

But that would have been an impulsive act, and Pop Merrill belonged to the Reasonable tribe—belonged to it body and soul, is what I mean to say. He didn't want to do anything on the spur of the moment that he might regret later, and—

If you don't do this, you'll regret it later.

But no. And no. And no. A man couldn't run against his nature. It was unnatural. He needed time to think.

To be sure. (711)

Pop becomes alert to the evil of the camera and is in a position to destroy it, but his choice to keep it for the selfish goals of either uncovering its secrets or reaping the profits of its sale results in his demise. His death comes after snapping the shutter the number of times needed to unleash the monster behind it.

While King often shows that those who reject their better intuitions sometimes fall, he balances his theory of the moral human condition by giving portrayals of heroes who defeat adversity when they choose to act with good will and kindness based on morality.

Irv Manders, the old man who offers temporary sanctuary to Andy and Charlie McGee, refugees from a government operation called The Shop, in the novel *Firestarter,* is a prime example. When Andy and his daughter, Charlie, come to Irv's farm while on the run from the agency that plans to apprehend them with the intent of using their supernatural powers for government research, Irv is placed in a situation where he can either recognize their troubles and give them aid or refuse to interfere in the business of others, as many people tend to do, and turn them over to the authorities seeking them. Irv chooses to protect Andy and Charlie and acts on their behalf when The Shop representatives arrive at his home. As Deborah Notkin explains, "Irv seems to personify King's faith, for he can take people on their own recognizance despite contrary evidence, can stand up for their rights as if his own were in jeopardy, and can shelter them without regard for his own danger" (140). It is Irv's refusal to surrender the well-being of Andy and Charlie that serves as an obstacle in The Shop's attempt at apprehension. It is also Irv's selflessness that serves as a reference for the good that may result when one human acts on behalf of another for the remainder of the book. Irv is the extreme opposite of the novel's chief antagonist, John Rainbird, a Shop employee who pretends to be concerned with Charlie but is only misleading her with the intent of winning her trust so that he can get close enough to her to kill her. Irv, on the other hand, is truly interested in her well-being and is willing to sacrifice his own welfare for her. By creating characters like Irv and Rainbird, King offers readers the opportunity to evaluate the two extremes of the moral human condition, and in so doing, allows readers to comprehend the power of good over evil that results from sincere concern for other living creatures. Notkin points out of King, "very few writers of contemporary fiction would even create such a simply good character as Irv Manders, let alone imply that he might be the rule rather than the exception" (141).

While Irv and Rainbird serve to illustrate the scope of moral action arising from a general concern for others, another main cause of King's characters' failure to act morally comes from a combination of their inability to recognize their own shortcomings and their subordination of their human intuition for rational reasoning. These human flaws are innate; it is much easier to rationalize problems by adhering to reason than to trace fault back to the original source, oneself. Only those characters in King's fiction who are able to assert their imperfections can possess the power to change themselves and ultimately act in defense of moral righteousness. Bosky argues that:

in King's fiction, natural human intuition is almost always correct and its results are often positive if followed—which it rarely is by the adult characters.Many of King's characters consistently refuse to trust their inner hunches, but there is usually at least one character in each story who does follow intuition, often with heroic results and probable, satisfying resolution. (212)

Those characters who acknowledge their weaknesses and trust their inner hunches, the ones innate in promoting the welfare of mankind, are those who acquire the power to fight evil. On the other hand, those characters who forsake intuition for human reasoning are those who are often incapacitated. The reason many of King's characters choose to ignore their intuition is that they have decided to shine a moral searchlight at others when what they really need to do is turn it back toward themselves. They believe in a rational explanation for everything that occurs as dictated by reason and have no faith in human individual choice, more specifically, their own choices. When acting on behalf of reason, they believe they cannot be wrong. Their subjective intuitions and impulses are almost always forfeited and subordinated to rational logic. In King's short story "I Am the Doorway," a story in *Night Shift*, it takes supernatural interference to show the protagonist, Arthur, that he is flawed. During an exploration of Venus, one of Arthur's crewmates ventures outside of the spacecraft. He comes back inside contaminated with an alien presence; that alien presence spreads to Arthur, who recognizes it later with the appearance of several tiny eyes that have been surfacing on his hands. The eyes ultimately force him to look inside of himself from an outsider's point of view:

It was a feeling like no other in the world—as if I were a portal just slightly ajar through which they were peeking at a world which they hated and feared. But the worst part was that I could see, too, in a way. Imagine your mind transported into a body of a housefly, a housefly looking into your own face with a thousand eyes. Then perhaps you can begin to see why I kept my hands bandaged even when there was no one around to see them. (97-98)

He says, describing the sensation received from the alien eyes in his hands: "But that was not what made me scream. I had looked into my own face and seen a monster" (101). Arthur, a representative of the common human being incapable of recognizing his own faults— one of the "Reasonable tribe"—needs the interference of an outside presence, a presence that is not human, to see that he is imperfect. A character like Arthur serves to reinforce one of King's general concerns about human beings—that personal introspection is sometimes impossible to achieve by oneself; the fact that King must create an outside supernatural force to hold up a moral mirror to Arthur's face should say something about King's recognition of some people's inability to evaluate themselves. Characters like *Pet Sematary*'s Louis Creed, *The Stand*'s Harold Lauder, *The Sun Dog*'s Pop Merrill, and *Christine*'s Arnie Cunningham—characters who aren't fortunate enough to benefit from an outside interference that causes them to question their own morality—are blunt examples of what happens in King's world when humans remain ignorant of their own shortcomings.

King's concept of moral degeneration arising from humans' indifference to their own flaws is not an original one. It is a theme that can be found throughout literature merely because of its universal truth; it does not apply solely to today's people and society but rather addresses the human condition as it has been throughout time. In drawing a comparison between King's protagonists and those created by other significant writers such as Herman Melville and Edgar Allen Poe, Tony Magistrale illustrates the universality of the idea:

There is a strong suggestion that Ahab and Poe's narrators secretly hate what they see to be a reflection of themselves found in the objects of their vengeance; for it is clear that in abandoning the most fundamental precepts of morality in order to accomodate the selfish urge to dominate and torment their fellow creatures, Ahab and Poe's narrators end up destroying themselves. (LOF 21)

As the passage serves to explicate, the failure of people to successfully investigate their own morality, resulting in a self-destructive projection of internal flaws onto an external embodiment of those flaws, has been recognized by authors for years. In King's canon, the recognition can often be found in his portrayal of an adult world that persecutes its young; King's adults often subliminally despise both the exposure to worldliness and the access to evil brought about by their physical and mental growth, and they project that hatred to those that they no longer are: the young and innocent (*It, The Body, The Library Policeman, The Talisman*). In *Stephen King: The Art of Darkness*, Douglas Winter also points out that moral degeneration from lack of introspection is not an original King concept:

King's plague of vampires, like that of Jack Finney's "body snatchers," is less an invasion than a sudden confirmation of what we have silently suspected all along: that we are taking over ourselves, individuals succumbing to the whole. The relentless process of fragmentation and isolation—a progressive degradation of individuals to a one-dimensional, spiritless mass—has seen the moral disintegration of an entire town [regarding 'Salem's Lot]. (47)

What Winter is referring to in citing 'Salem's Lot is a town of people who are so busy finding faults in their neighbors that they are not able to unite in battle against the vampires that are preying upon them. The novel is not so much about vampires as it is about the fall of a community resulting from a breach of faith among brothers and sisters. King often details in the novel the ludicrousness of the exchanges between 'Salem's Lot's citizens. Rather than utilizing their energies to identify and change their own imperfections, they highlight those of others. These tendencies culminate in a state of isolation, denying any form of human bonding in the struggle, culminating in a complete lack of community action. The citizens have not been destroyed by vampires as much as they have destroyed themselves because of their inability to change and correct their own lives through moral maturity.

What English fiction, horror fiction, and specifically Stephen King's fiction have to teach their readers is that the first step toward mental maturity is gaining an understanding of the impact each and every person's moral standing has on the rest of society. As real monsters such as Ted Bundy and Jeffrey Dahmer have shown, even one person's breach of morality can affect the lives of an entire city or nation. Once an individual has learned the consequences of choice, learned to share the self with others, learned to see one's personal shortcomings, learned to believe in the good residing in the human spirit, then he or she will have taken a step toward becoming whole that may be more significant than any other emotional development imaginable. The fictitious characters Stephen King creates serve to present to King's readers images of themselves, calling to question issues of their own morality.

II. Childhood and Rites of Passage

The child in adult life is defenceless
And if he is grown-up, knows it,
And the grown-up looks at the childish part
And despises it.

Stevie Smith
"To Carry the Child"

Anyone who has read Stephen King extensively will find that he spends a large amount of time exploring childhood. Childhood to King is a magical time, a time when the world seems magnificent in its literal beauty, a time when a human being is most splendid because of ignorance of worldly evil. King recollects with fondness an age when imaginative capacities are boundless because they are not yet bogged down by the spirit-corrupting concerns of adulthood. This preoccupation with youth in his fiction becomes both significant and inspirational when seen from the light that King is writing in an America that attempts to desensitize its young by exposing it continuously to violence and sex in both the entertainment and news media, forcing it to mature at too early an age. Children to King are like lumps of clay on a potter's wheel waiting to be sculpted into the individuals they will later become; they are the most impressionable beings in the human chain.

While they begin innocent, not yet concerned with how they look or where they will get money to buy a new car, children still are forced at some point to exit the gates of purity and enter the arena of adulthood, which occurs through some initial earth-shattering discovery that causes them to recognize the imperfections of their world. For some children, the initiation may be discovering that their fathers are not the spotless, faultless men they thought they were but rather pathetic alcoholics. Others may find their untainted visions of their world clouded by a first exposure to a pornographic magazine depicting radically different images of sexuality than those which they'd been taught. King revels in both the pre-corrupted and corrupted states of youth. He feels that they are periods that people must return to in later years to complete the wheel of humanity; if people cannot remember both the magic of childhood before its corruption and the lessons learned during and after its corruption, then they will never be complete but will succumb to the evils of the adult world.

First and foremost of King's fascination with children is the imaginative capacity they have that makes them stronger at heart than the adults who claim superiority over them. While adults claim to be wise, they are ignorant to the fact that the imaginative atrophy often resulting from an inability to adapt to innocence's corruption actually limits them. Adults often can no longer discover the beauty in a sunset; they cannot remember the golden moments of childhood bonding, a period when same-sex friends seemed the most important aspect of being alive, and it is this incapacity to recollect these times that often leads to an increasingly burdensome adult life in King's fiction. Unless the adults in King's world can escape into the realm of imagination first experienced and shared with others in childhood, unless they can approach oncoming evil with a child's mentality, they are doomed to adult reasoning. Because evil in itself is intangible and cannot be reasonably rationalized, it is often both adults' adherence to their belief in reason and their insistency on literalizing reality and unreality that often result in a catastrophe in King's fiction. Only when they open themselves up to combatting evil from a child's perspective, one which believes in monsters and ghosts, can they openly battle adversities.

King's interest in children's imagination could be linked directly to his feelings on moral choice discussed previously. Adults are unable to see their shortcomings because they are too enveloped in a subjectively egocentric universe based on the rules of rationality. A child, who is ever open to the threats of vampires, killer cars, haunted hotels, and killer clowns, is not yet able to reject the thought of entering the world of the irrational. Clive Barker, one of King's leading contemporaries in horror fiction, says of King, "In King's work, it is so often the child who carries that wisdom; the child who synthesizes 'real' and 'imagined' experience without question, who knows instinctively that imagination can tell the truth the way the senses never can" (63). Often in King's books, it takes the imagination of a child to cast away the evil that reduces adults to whimpering fools: *It*'s The Loser's Club, a group of socially outcast children who possess the imaginative capacities to recognize the evil plundering Derry and therefore acquire the power to stop it; *'Salem's Lot*'s Mark Petrie, whose belief in the world of monsters allows protagonist Ben Mears to return to his own childhood fears which upon retrospection provide him with the power to combat the vampires quenching their thirsts on the small town; *The Shining's* Danny Torrance, whose childish imagination provides a welcome birthplace for supernatural powers capable of turning back the all-consuming evil of the hotel that has claimed his father; and *The Talisman's* Jack Sawyer, who because of his youth and separation from the adult world of reasoning becomes his ailing mother's savior while an evil adult society led by his malicious Uncle Morgan tries to destroy them both. The child heroes in King's fiction continue to increase, merely because of King's awareness that their innocence is the only hope for survival in an unimaginative adult world that is swallowing itself.

King often highlights the plight of American children by portraying an adult society that is trying to soil its young by stealing their purity. The sad truth lies in the fact that while children are stronger than their elders in their ability to utilize their imaginations in the face of adversities, they are incapacitated by their dependency on adults. As a result, adults possess the power to make lasting impressions—often negative ones—on their young simply because of both their physical superiority and worldly mentality, something Bernadette Lynn Bosky points out:

Children do not resist their impressions partly because they have not learned adult standards of sanity and already exist in a shocking and primal world that adults can barely recall or comprehend. It is a sad irony, exampled in books like *The Shining*, *Cujo*, and *Pet Sematary*, that children, who often understand the intrinsics of evil best, have the least power to change it. (216)

While children basically possess the true weapons for survival—a productive imagination, a love for simple things, a gentle nature—they are often made vulnerable by an adult society that teaches them violence, hostility, and greed. In their vulnerability, children become sponges that absorb the impressions their adult society gives them, which King himself explains:

What is it about kids that they can look at the most outrageous thing and just see it and, unless there's a reaction they can play off, just deal with it? If a kid sees a guy that's dead in the street, who's been hit by a car, if he's by himself he'll just look at the dead guy and then maybe run off to find somebody—after he'd had a good look to see what it was like. But if a lot of people are standing around crying, then the kid will cry too, because he's got a mirror reaction. Kids by themselves sort of interest me that way; they seem to me to be the place where you should start to explore wherever people come from. (BB 105)

As King suggests, children learn from the adult reactions to which they are exposed. King's fiction which deals with the gap between young and old tends to argue that the negative responses children register from adults are those that are most often recollected later in adult life, serving as a basis for chronic human flaws. In *The Library Policeman*, a novella in *Four Past Midnight*, King speaks this observation through Dirty Dave Duncan's mouth:

I don't think kids know monsters so well at first glance. It's their folks that tell em how to recognize the monsters.... And when they went home [from Ardelia Lortz's terrifying renditions of fairy tales], they didn't remember, in the top part of their minds, anyways, about the stories or the posters. Down underneath, I think they remembered plenty, just like down underneath Sam knows who his Library Policeman is. I think they still remember today—the bankers and lawyers and big-time farmers who were once Ardelia's Good Babies. I can still see em, wearin pinafores and short pants, sittin in those little chairs, lookin at Ardelia in the middle of the circle, their eyes so big and round they looked like pie-plates. And I think that when it gets dark and the storms come, or when they are sleepin and the nightmares come, they go back to bein kids. I think the doors open and they see the Three Bears—Ardelia's Three Bears—eatin the brains out of Goldilock's head with their wooden porridge-spoons, and Baby Bear wearin Goldilock's scalp on his head like a long golden wig. I think they wake up sweaty, feelin sick and afraid. I think that's what she left this town. I think she left a legacy of secret nightmares. (527)

The Ardelia Lortz that Dirty Dave speaks of is a stain on his memories. She is the embodiment of the adult world that strives to swallow its young. In the past, she had run the public library in town where children's readings took place. Once the doors were shut and the parents had gone, Ardelia perverted all of the children's favorite fairy tales into her own gory versions where the protagonists are killed and maimed because they are naughty little children. When the listeners showed fear, she took them into another room and turned into a monster with a funnel-shaped mouth that sucked the tears of fear right from their eyes; she sucked them dry of all the imaginative capabilities that kept them young, staining their youth with her corrupted adult vision.

Ardelia is central to the story because it is she who comes back as a ghost to feed on protagonist Sam Peebles' fear, one which was never resolved as a child. Sam's fear is of libraries; what once were places of limitless possiblities, places of magical learning, are now to Sam the manifestations of a dark memory from past years—the memory of being raped by a homosexual child molester when Sam was returning an overdue book to the public library. The child molester had claimed that he was punishing Sam for being a naughty boy who did not return his book on time. The young Sam, who, like children everywhere, was impressionable in his youth, took the molester's accusation to heart, and from that point on, had his childish fascination with libraries reduced to repulsion. Dirty Dave, who had followed Ardelia's persecution of the young when she was living primarily because of an adult lust for her, also admits that corrupting children was appealing to his adult mind:

There's a part of me, even now, that wants to sugarcoat it, make my part in it better than it was. I'd like to tell you that I fought with her, argued, told her I didn't want nothin to do with scarin a bunch of kids...but it wouldn't be true. I went right along with what she wanted me to do. God help me, I did. Partly it was because I was scared of her by then. But mostly it was because I was still besotted with her. And there was something else, too. There was a mean, nasty part of me—I don't think it's in everyone, but I think it's in a lot of us—that liked what she was up to. Liked it. (520)

The combination of supplicating himself for Ardelia's body and secretly enjoying the corruption of youth alienates Dirty Dave from the children whom he had respected and admired prior to meeting Ardelia. His feelings about the role he played in Ardelia's perversion of Junction City's children is significant when put together with the other adults in the story who thrive on eradicating the magic of youth, a tendency in adults that Sam has difficulty understanding, keeping him from being whole. Because Sam Peebles had never been able to come to terms with the reality of his perversion, he cannot defeat Ardelia and the Library Policeman of his past until he can return to his childhood and retrieve the golden moments that were stolen from him.

Prior to being raped, Sam had purchased a pack of red licorice. The red licorice, like the library, had become a negative memory, one that prior to his manipulation by the molester had been a meaningful token of his youth. Sam defeats Ardelia and the Library Policeman by buying several packs of the same red licorice and jamming them into the mouth of the monster—which ultimately becomes a union of Ardelia, his molester, and all the negative memories those adults represent—that is trying to swallow him the same way it did his innocence. Because he is finally able to return to the magic of his childhood, using those memories to oppose his enemies, the adult Sam is able to reclaim a portion of the innocence that the adult world had taken from him.

King's stories that depict a conflict between children and adults may be seen as having their foundations built in the portrayal of the age gap as presented by the American media. Television and movies often portray the young as threatening to the adult world, something easily identified in films such as *The Exorcist*, a story about a young girl who, after being possessed by the devil, strikes out at the adults surrounding her; *The Omen*, which uses a child as the vehicle through which the coming of the Beast as promised in the book of Revelations is realized; *The Class of 1984*, a film that tells the story of a man's battle against a group of delinquent high school students who represent all of the destructive impulses in humankind; and the number of movies that portray youths and adolescents as wanting nothing but a good time void of responsibility—drinking, getting high, playing rock music, wanting constant sex (*Porky's*, *Friday the 13th*, *Fast Times at Ridgemont High*). The media has indeed tended to condition society into believing that the young are a threat to the adult world's standards of living. By presenting youths in such a fashion, the media has succeeded in stereotyping them. While these presentations may be seen on one side as reactions by youths who are fighting against their elders who are suppressing them, most often they are viewed as the mirror opposite: the young lack respect for the old and therefore suffer in failing to adhere to adult precepts. The sad truth lies in the fact that the media, which is run by adults, often does not look back on adolescence as a meaningful time but rather focuses on the tragedies that occur during youth: a painful loss of virginity, illicit experimentation with controlled substancies resulting in negative consequences, painful pranks on vulnerable peers. Instead of portraying children and adolescents as having the strength and imaginative capacities to combat their adversities, American media has often presented them as weak, disturbed individuals with ambiguous identities who perish because of their helplessness and lack of moral direction.

King seems to be aware of the misinterpretation of the young in the media, and he tries to provide an alternative viewpoint by portraying his young people as being stronger than the corrupt adult world. Often in his books, the initial coming of age occurs when children first become wise to the several rites of initiation into adulthood offered by their elders. The optimism King has for American youth shines through in his belief that children have the capacity to achieve mature growth when passing through these rites of passage; more often than not, King's young people are able to leave their states of innocence with their heads held high and are strong enough to recognize the significance of the step in human development they are taking. In *The Sun Dog*, Kevin Delevan, the young owner of the Polaroid Sun 660 that so captivates Pop Merrill's attention, has the strength to determine when he will be ready to cross the line separating purity from experience, an ability to discriminate that shines clear in his recollection of a hunting trip with his father:

Bet you wish it'd been your turn in the puckies, don't you, son? the game-warden had asked, ruffling Kevin's hair. Kevin had nodded, keeping his secret to himself: he was glad it hadn't been his turn in the puckies, his rifle which must be responsible for throwing the slug or not throwing it...and, if he had turned out to have the courage to do the shooting, his reward would have been only another troublesome responsibility: to shoot the buck clean. He didn't know if he could have mustered the courage to put another bullet in the thing if the kill wasn't clean, or the strength to chase the trail of its blood and steaming, startled droppings and finish what he started if it ran. He had smiled up at the game-warden and nodded and his dad had snapped a picture of that, and there had never been any need to tell his dad that the thought going on behind that upturned brow and under the game-warden's ruffling hand had been No. I don't wish it. The world is full of tests, but twelve's too young to go hunting them. I'm glad it was Mr. Roberson. I'm not ready yet to try a man's tests. (756)

These reflections take place when Kevin is facing the dog that Pop Merrill had released from the camera because of his greedy adult anxiety. This is a turning point in the story because it is this moment when Kevin must decide whether to turn the camera that will be used to combat the dog over to his father or whether to take on the task himself, a man's task that he had not yet been prepared to face while hunting at the age of twelve. Kevin recognizes that the present moment is the time to make that step, for where before crossing into manhood would have been done in vain (shooting a deer), he is now in a position to save both his and his father's lives:

The thought of turning the Polaroid over to his father crossed his mind, but only momentarily. Something deep inside himself knew the truth: to pass the camera would be tantamount to murdering his father and committing suicide himself. His father believed something, but that wasn't specific enough. The camera wouldn't work for his father even if his father managed to break out of his current stunned condition and press the shutter. It would only work for him. (757)

After recalling the time when he was tempted to enter the adult world, a transition that could have been accomplished by aiming his rifle at the deer and mortally wounding it, Kevin remembers that he had in his heart resisted the temptation, knowing truly well he was not yet ready. The coming of age into adulthood occurs when he realizes that he is in a position to react like an adult, yet the magic of the transition rests in the fact that Kevin also understands that he is not stained because of this awareness but rather is in close enough contact with his youth to have the imaginative capacity to defeat the inexplicable atrocity bearing down on him and his father. While recognizing that his father is slightly aware of what is going on as the dog prepares to strike, Kevin has the inner strength to speculate that his father is still too out of touch with such phenomena because of the imaginative atrophy of adulthood. The combined abilities to walk through his rite of passage with confidence and utilize his childish capacities result in Kevin's life-saving effort.

The Body, King's tour de force of coming of age stories, also portrays young people as having the inner strength to make the transition from innocence to experience. After hearing of a boy from town who had disappeared after venturing out to pick berries, a group of four young boys embark on a journey through miles of railroad tracks and vegetation to find the boy, who they believe is surely dead. Along the trip, the four begin to realize the significance of their union in their search and are able to grasp the splendor of childhood bonding, which provides the catapult to accomplishing their task. Gordie Lachance, the story's narrator, acts as spokesperson for the group when he explicates his growing realization that both he and his friends are taking a significant step toward maturity in searching a first exposure to death:

Unspoken—maybe it was too fundamental to be spoken—was the idea that this was a big thing. It wasn't screwing around with firecrackers or trying to look through the knothole in the back of the girls' privy at Harrison State Park. This was something on a par with getting laid for the first time, or going into the Army, or buying your first bottle of legal liquor.

There's a high ritual to all fundamental events, the rites of passage, the magic corridor where the change happens. Buying the condoms. Standing before the minister. Raising your hand and taking the oath. Or, if you please, walking down the railroad tracks to meet a fellow your own age halfway, the same as I'd walk half-way over to Pine Street to meet Chris if he was coming over to my house, or the way Teddy would walk halfway down Gates Street to meet me if I was going to his. It seemed right to do it this way, because the rite of passage is a magic corridor and so we always provide an aisle—it's what you walk down when you get married, what they carry you down when you get buried. Our corridor was those twin rails, and we walked between them, just bopping along toward whatever this was supposed to mean. (415)

Gordie's passage suggests that he and his friends have reached a point where they are prepared to traverse into the world of experience, leaving their innocence behind. The passage is inspirational in that it does not portray youth teetering on the "unstable legs of adolescence" but rather suggests that the boys are indeed ready to make the transition confidently. In the end, they are able to complete their rite of passage with authority. After they discover the dead body, a group of older boys wanting media exposure burst in to claim the body for themselves. The younger ones, realizing the trials they had to endure in achieving their end goal, use their accumulated strength to turn the interlopers back. Once again, King has presented a vision of youth that has the capacity to grow from change and heed the lessons it provides.

King also attempts to show in his fiction that children and adolescents are not always the blank slates that adults believe them to be. While King's adults boast a knowledge of the world, they are often ignorant of the fact that their intimate relationship with rational explanation gives them less an understanding of the line separating reality from unreality that youths in their imaginative splendor can access. King's young people, while still innocent, are indeed often aware that there are some things that they can comprehend that their elders could not even if they tried. In effect, it is the imaginative capacities that King's children possess that ultimately alienate them from adults. A scene from 'Salem's Lot that supports this idea: upon arriving home after visiting the Marsten house, where he hears the voice of head-vampire Barlow in the cellar, young Mark Petrie is greeted with dismay by his parents, who have been worried sick over his extended absence:

"Where have you been?" She caught his shoulders and shook them.
"Out," he said wanly. "I fell down running home."
There was nothing else to say. The essential and defining characterstic of childhood is not the effortless merging of dream and reality, but only alienation. There are no words for childhood's dark turns and exhalations. A wise child recognizes it and submits to the necessary consequences. A child who counts the cost is a child no longer.
He added: "The time got away from me. It—"
Then his father, descending upon him. (293)

Mark Petrie comes home looking like he'd just been run over by a car, an appearance caused by his stumbling and falling while running from the Marsten house. But he cannot tell his parents the truth, because in their adult tendency to adhere to reason, they could not possibly understand or believe him. Mark understands and endures the ensuing interrogation.

Other examples of a child's interpretation of the world as opposed to an adult's can be found throughout King's canon. In *The Library Policeman*, Sam Peebles begins to make the distinction after observing a grim poster Ardelia Lortz had put up on the door to the children's reading room in the public library:

The door was closed. On it was a picture of Little Red Riding Hood, looking down at the wolf in grandma's bed. The wolf was wearing Grandma's nightgown and Grandma's nightcap. It was snarling. Foam dripped from between its bared fangs. An expression of almost exquisite horror had transfixed Little Red Riding Hood's face, and the poster seemed not just to suggest but to actually proclaim that the happy ending of this story—of all fairy tales—was a convenient lie. Parents might believe such guff, Red Riding Hood's ghastly-sick face said, but the little ones knew better, didn't they? (418)

Peebles recognizes during a retrospect on childhood that there are some things that children can see in their vivid imaginations that adults, members of the "Reasonable tribe" never could. Likewise, in the short story "The Boogeyman" (*Night Shift*), protagonist Lester Billings begins to grasp his own lack of childish imagination that, had it been present, may have saved his children from the monster preying on them from their closets:

I started to think, maybe if you think of a thing long enough, believe in it, it gets real. Maybe all the monsters we were scared of when we were kids, Frankenstein and Wolfman and Mummy, maybe they were real. Real enough to kill the kids they said fell in gravel pits or drowned in lakes or were just never found. Maybe grownups unmake that world because we're so sure of the world's normalcy. ("The Boogeyman," Fogler Special Collections 6)

Up until this point, Billings had reprimanded his children for dreaming up the monster in their closets. Because of the separation between what his children believed and what he was not able to believe, Billing's ignorance ends in their deaths. The children who were able to understand the world of monsters were completely helpless to stop the one living among them; their only savior, their father, did not have the imaginative capacity to heed their call of distress. (Note: "The Boogeyman" is also interesting in its implications of an adult world persecuting its young. Billing's disbelief of the monster in his house also arises from his hostility toward his children, who, rather than being seen as a blessing, are seen as extra baggage. Prior to his children's deaths, Billings had come to think of his children as unwanted responsibilities. In effect, what Billings denies to be the cause of his children's deaths also arises from his subconscious desire to see himself rid of them.)

Although King often attempts to explain the imaginative capacities that separate the young from the old, thereby making children better prepared in the shadow of oncoming danger, he does not make children completely spotless in their understandings of the human condition. On the contrary, while King writes to show the differences between the imaginations of the young and old, he also explicates that there are certain awarenesses to which adults have access while children do not. From this perspective, while a child is often aware of an adult's misunderstanding of the supernatural and imaginable realm, an adult is cognizant of a child's inability to estimate human nature. This concept would tend to argue that a child, who has not yet been exposed enough to the evil ways in which the world operates, is vulnerable in his or her ignorance of adult human behavior. The following exchange between Andy McGee and his daughter, Charlie, in *Firestarter* suggests this important differential between an adult's understanding of the world as compared to a child's:

[at a Best Western hotel after Andy has rescued Charlie from The Shop agents who have just executed his wife]

"I want Mommy," she sobbed.

He nodded. He wanted her, too. He held Charlie tightly to him and smelled ozone and porcelain and cooked Best Western towels. She had almost flashfried them both.

"It's gonna be all right," he told her, and rocked her, not really believing it, but it was the litany, the Psalter, the voice of the adult calling down the black well of years into the miserable pit of terrorized childhood; it was what you said when things went wrong; it was the nightlight that could not banish the monster from the closet but perhaps only keep it at bay for a little while; it was the voice without power that must speak nevertheless.

"It's gonna be all right," he told her, not really believing it, knowing as every adult knows in his secret heart that nothing is really all right, ever. "It's gonna be all right."

He was crying. He couldn't help it now. His tears came in a flood and he held her to his chest as tightly as he could.

"Charlie, I swear to you, somehow it's gonna be all right." (180)

The difference in worldly knowledge between children and adults is apparent in the novel. Charlie possesses the talent of pyrokinesis, which enables her to set fires at will. Her understanding of her talent is representative of a young child's: she does not yet understand the power she holds within her, and she is often left in a state of disorientation after she uses it. Too young to understand controlling it, Charlie only uses the power, much as any young child would, spontaneously; she only uses it when either she or her father is in danger. The adult world, on the other hand, wants to use her as a secret governmental weapon. Because they recognize the massive destruction Charlie's power can inflict, the adult world (represented as The Shop and the U.S. government) tries to apprehend her and harness her wild talent. In her youth, Charlie is too young to understand that adults wish to manipulate her, much as she is too young to realize that things are not "all right"—a consolation that her father must prevericate to ease her tension. Only Andy, a grown-up member of the adult society, possesses this understanding that will take years for his daughter to comprehend.

King's analysis of youth does not end with pre-adolescent childhood. On the contrary, he spends an equal amount of text exploring life after the initial coming of age, which takes place after children have lost their innocence through an initiation to worldliness. He is just as concerned with the next stage of human development, adolescence, which actually serves as the void between the extremities of childhood innocence and adult experience.

Adolescence to King may be the most turbulent period of people's lives because it is a time when they must develop their personalities without any firm ground to stand on; no longer wearing the pure skin of childhood, yet also not bearing the experienced colors of adulthood, adolescents are often trapped in identity crises. The development that takes place during this period carries tremendous implications concerning what people will become as adults. Susceptible to confusion about themselves, King's adolescents are vulnerable to adversity. Douglas Winter, quoting author Charles L. Grant, indicates King's preoccupation with adolescence by arguing, "In King's view, 'the struggle toward adolescence and adulthood is as fraught with terror as the worst possible nightmare, and as meaningful as anything a grown-up has to contend with' " (SK 32). Critic Tom Newhouse provides what is perhaps the most accurate description of the dilemma facing King's adolescents when he writes that "they are often outsiders who turn to violence as a response to exclusionary social environments which deny them acceptance, or who resort to destructive attitudes that they believe will advance them upward" (49). While a student at the University of Maine at Orono, King wrote a weekly column titled "King's Garbage Truck," which appeared in the campus newspaper, *The Maine Campus*. In his May 21, 1970, column, the last "Garbage Truck" column he wrote, King said this about his own transition into the adult world after completing his required studies:

This boy has shown evidences of some talent, although at this point it is impossible to tell if he is just a flash in the pan or if he has real possibilities. It seems obvious that he has learned a great deal at the University of Maine at Orono, although a great deal has contributed to a lessening of idealistic fervor rather than a heightening of that characteristic. If a speaker at his birth into the real world mentions "changing the world with the bright-eyed vigor of youth" this young man is apt to flip him the bird and walk out, as he does not feel very bright-eyed by this time; in fact, he feels about two thousand years old.

It is implicit in this statement that even King, who when he wrote this was writing non-fiction, was weary of the tasks that lay ahead of him in making the complete transition to adulthood. Perhaps it is a realization such as this one that has been the motivating factor behind devoting a large portion of his literature to the uphill battle young people must endure when struggling through the crises brought about by fighting to understand who they are.

Finding a meaningful identity is perhaps the most pervasive conflict facing King's fictitious adolescents. The vulnerability arising from having no sound identity often opens them up to the constant fire of adversities being cast at them by adults and peers alike. No better example can be found than in King's first published novel, *Carrie*. *Carrie* is the story of an ugly-duckling with an extraordinary gift, telekinesis, which enables her to move stationary objects by merely using her will. She is simultaneously persecuted by her peers, who take advantage of her humble docility, and her religious fundamentalist mother, who interprets everything Carrie does as being sinful. While trying to discover her identity, Carrie's view of herself is continuously distorted by the ways in which her immediate associates react to her. Winter argues that "she is at the center of an ever-tightening circle of control, of a society laden with traps that demand conformity and the loss of identity" (35). Her significant others seem intent on dictating to Carrie exactly how she is to view herself. Yet while she is discouraged from asserting herself as an autonomous individual, she carries on with the human desire to persevere. She is granted the opportunity to grasp her femininity when a classmate, Sue Snell, takes pity on her after succumbing to the guilt from her involvement in taunting Carrie and forfeits her prom date, Tommy Ross, whom she persuades to escort Carrie to the dance. Carrie reacts to the invitation by making herself up, allowing her natural beauty hidden beneath her humble exterior to shine through, which stuns her adversaries. The peers most preoccupied with making Carrie's life a living hell respond by dumping pig blood on her when she is mockingly elected prom queen. When she returns home after wreaking destruction on those who shamed her, she walks into the second trap, her mother, who, believing Carrie had been out behaving immorally, rebukes her. Like Carrie's peers, her mother ultimately dies at the hand of Carrie's wrath. The results of prom night are catastrophic, and the tragedy lies in the fact that Carrie had finally summoned the courage to exercise her autonomy only to have her peers and her mother deny her that opportunity.

Carrie is metamorphasized into a monster by the society that tried to repress her. But all the while, the reader never truly views Carrie as an atrocity; on the contrary, she demands the reader's sympathy. She does not willfully conduct evil against others but rather is forced to lash back at those who try consistently to eradicate the one thing that has any significant meaning in Carrie's adolescence: her self-worth. Critic Ben Indick explains King's treatment of Carrie as a victim rather than as an aggressor when he says that "the heroine of *Carrie*, no more mature than most of her fellow teenagers, nevertheless tries to understand herself and particularly her mother. Her destructive acts come only because she has no way to respond emotionally and intellectually" (160).

Another prime example of a King adolescent who is pushed into mayhem is Arnie Cunningham in *Christine*. Arnie is the male counterpart of Carrie. While he does not possess any wild talent, he is similar to Carrie in his awkwardness and forced humility because of his lack of physical prowess. Like Carrie's peers, Arnie's never accept him but insist on keeping him humble. Girls will have nothing to do with him, thinking he is a geek with zits. Boys intimidate him because he is weak. Arnie even feels alienated from his parents, who expect him to follow the blueprint of his life they have drawn for him. When Arnie finds and purchases Christine, a '57 Plymouth Fury in which he takes great pride, his feelings of persecution are reinforced from all sides: his parents reject the car because they think it will keep him from his studies, and his peers react with distaste because they realize his fixation with it has made him bolder in his stand against them. His parents discourage his involvement with the car by prohibiting him from parking it in front of the house, and his teenage adversaries at one point pulverize it. Aside from Dennis Guilder, Arnie's one true friend, Arnie is under constant pressure to refrain from establishing any meaningful identity of his own—an identity he feels the car could provide. Dennis summarizes Arnie's plight and that of any other high school outcast when he says that:

he was a loser, you know. Every high school has to have at least two; it's like a national law. One male, one female. Everyone's dumping ground. Having a bad day? Flunked a big test? Had an argument with your folks and got grounded for the weekend? No problem. Just find one of those poor sad sacks that go scurrying around the halls like criminals before the home-room bell and walk it right to him. (1)

In effect, Arnie comes to believe that his only purposes in life are to play both the punching bag on which his peers take out their frustrations and the obedient son who must respect his parents' wishes, even if those wishes conflict with his own.

As Arnie's attachment to Christine grows stronger, so do the lines separating Arnie from his significant others grow clearer. In an exchange with Dennis, Arnie discloses his unhappiness with his parents, a feeling not unfamiliar to many adolescents:

"Has it ever occurred to you," he said abruptly, "that parents are nothing but overgrown kids until their children drag them into adulthood? Usually kicking and screaming?"

I shook my head.

"Tell you what I think," he said "I think that part of being a parent is trying to kill your kids. I know it sounds a little crazy at first...but there are lots of things that sound nuts until you really consider them. Penis envy. Oedpial conflicts. The Shroud of Turin...I really believe it, though...not that they know what they're doing; I don't believe that at all. And do you know why?...Because as soon as you have a kid, you know for sure that you're going to die. When you have a kid, you see your own gravestone." (26-27)

Arnie's feelings of no way out—his despair in establishing a positive meaningful identity while under fire from significant others—combined with his lack of faith in people willing to form substantial relationships with him lead to his fall from humanity and susceptibility to evil. As Bernadette Lynn Bosky brings to light, "Arnie's feelings of great potential hidden by ugliness, of being unappreciated and socially excluded, pave the way for his seduction by Christine" (227). While Arnie does begin to understand Christine's evil late in the book, he still rejects the option to do the right thing—to destroy her—because he is unwilling to surrender the feelings of self-worth she has given him. Though he makes a severe lapse in moral judgment, it could be argued that he has been conditioned by the society persecuting him to dismiss any notion of brotherhood. In the end, Arnie, like Carrie White, can be observed as a sympathetic character even in the shadow of the mass destruction he causes because his downfall is the result of being denied his autonomy.

While King often expresses his sympathies for children and adolescents who are persecuted by a suppressive society comprised chiefly of adults, readers must not overlook that King is also making a call to adults that they may redeem themselves by thoughtfully looking back on their own youth and remembering the magic of those times and the lessons learned. What King is most concerned with in adults is their ability to complete a wheel: to begin life as innocent beings who are eventually corrupted by worldly evil who may then circle back to the period of innocence so that they may not lose touch with beauty of the human experience. Says King, "I'm interested in the notion of finishing off one's childhood as one completes making a wheel. The idea is to go back and confront your childhood, in a sense relive it if you can, so that you can be whole" (Winter, AOD 185). King fears that too often adults become so enveloped in the trials and tribulations of adult life that they drown themselves in the pools of logic and reason; in doing so, they forget the wonder of viewing the splendor and mysticism of life as seen through a child's eyes, an experience they must return to time and time again if they want to avoid being swallowed by the world:

Rather than indulge in a spurious attempt to recapture a social milieu, King's fiction often looks to our youth as the earlier way of life whose "swan song" must be sung. His stories are songs of innocence and experience, juxtaposing childhood and adulthood—effectively completing the wheel whose turn began in childhood by reexperiencing those days from a mature perspective. (Winter, AOD 10)

Often in King's fiction, the dilemma facing the adult characters stems directly from two inabilities. The first is the inability to return to childhood and remember the magic of those moments. The second is the failure to understand the significance of an event that happened during that time period—an event that is repressed rather than resolved as one grows older. King attempts to point out that there must be a synthesis between childhood and adult experiences—that one must be able to interpret life by merging the sensory and emotional input that occurs throughout the cycle of one's life. In *The Library Policeman*, the main conflict arises from Sam Peebles' initial inability to return to his childhood and face the atrocity (a homosexual rape) that was dealt to him then. Until the end of the story, instead of going back and facing what happened to him from a mature perspective, Sam hides the memory far back in his mind. But without the synthesis between childhood and adulthood, he is never really whole. Rather, he finds himself trapped solely in one period or the other, as adults can tend to do:

[after the Library Policeman has stormed into Sam's house]
Sam felt a triple-locked door far back in his mind straining to burst open. He never thought of running. The idea of flight was beyond his capacity to imagine. He was a child again, a child who has been caught red-handed
(the book isn't *The Speaker's Companion*) doing some awful bad thing. Instead of running (the book isn't *Best Loved Poems of the American People*)
he folded slowly over his own wet crotch and collapsed between the two stools which stood at the counter, holding his hands up blindly above his head. (487)

The reason the Library Policeman has come after Sam again is because Sam had recently failed to return two library books. Yet while Sam is cowering in the corner of his kitchen under the shadow of his intruder, the emotional salad being tossed in his brain tries to remind him that it is not only those two books for which his intruder has come back; to Sam, the Library Policeman is also asking once again for the Robert Louis Stevenson book he'd not returned as a child on the day the man raped him. Sam is bounced back and forth between the two time periods because he has not yet been able to complete the wheel and understand what had happened to him. Only when he is able to accomplish that circling back to his younger days can Sam efficiently battle his adversary. As Naomi Higgins, Sam's girlfriend, acknowledges when observing Sam's revival of spirit in confronting his enemy, "he looks like a man who has been granted the opportunity to return to his worst nightmares...with some powerful weapon in his hands" (576).

A similar situation can be found in 'Salem's Lot, where protagonist Ben Mears has returned to the town of his childhood carrying some heavy emotional baggage. When a youth, Ben had entered the Marsten house on a dare, and, after entering, had found the house's owner hanging by his neck from a support beam in an upstairs bedroom. Mears had fled from the house then and has returned to the present with that trauma still unresolved. This lack of resolve in understanding death is intensified by the recent death of his wife, who was killed in a fatal motorcycle accident in which Ben had been driving. Ben's predicament exists until he benefits from the aid of a child, Mark Petrie, who becomes the connection with childhood Ben needs in returning back to his own youth to understand death and dying. Ben then becomes emotionally equipped to combat the league of vampires presently spreading death throughout 'Salem's Lot once he is able to complete the wheel joining youth and adulthood.

What both Sam and Ben do in the end of their stories—complete the wheel—is elemental to King's understanding of the life cycle:

None of us adults remember childhood. We think we remember it, which is even more dangerous. Colors are brighter. The sky looks bigger. It's impossible to remember exactly how it was. Kids live in a constant state of shock. The input is so fresh and so strong that it's bound to be frightening. (BB 95)

As King points out, because the input is so powerful when perceived as a child, it becomes all the more difficult to recollect it as years separate adults from that experience. By making a mental effort to return to those days and recognizing the distance from them created by time, adults can capitalize on magical childhood moments by synthesizing the memory with an adult's perspective of life. King revealed this belief years before his first published novel in the March 27, 1969, "King's Garbage Truck," written at age 21: "Somehow everything seems to get just a little dirtier and more selfish as we get older. It's good to remember other times, once in a while. We'll have to do it again some time." Once adults can accomplish the synthesis, they will have taken a giant step toward becoming whole.

The need for adults to access their childhood and adolescent memories and observations resonates throughout King's fiction, published and unpublished. *Blaze*, an unpublished King novel held by the Raymond H. Fogler Library Special Collections Department at UMO, is a fine example. The story is about the life of Claiborne Blaisdell, Jr., an oversized man who has a history of criminal behavior in his adult years. Once a promising student as a youngster, his intellectual capacities were destroyed after a brain injury resulting from being thrown down a flight of stairs by his father. The injury caused Blaze's brain to slow, keeping his mind perpetually adolescent. His actions as an adult are correlative to a young person's for he is not cursed with the adult tendency to cheat and deceive. However, his limited intellect often leads to his manipulation and persecution. In order to console himself about the evil of the adult world, he reflects on memories such as the following, a time when he and a friend from the orphanage where he'd been raised played hookie to travel to Boston:

and they began to laugh with each other, laughing into each other's faces in a rare moment of triumph that comes only once or twice in the richest of lifetimes, a time that seems wholly natural and right when it occurs, but is golden and soft in retrospect, too beautiful to be looked at often. It is a time that is usually recalled in future circumstances that are bitter, a time that is wholly childhood, often painful in late-remembered truth. Blaze never forgot it. (70)

The story creates a valid argument that Blaze's slowed mental growth is a blessing in disguise. It allows him to see life continuously from a child's perspective which enables him to view simple things with wonder and imagination. The best example of this can be found in Blaze's attachment to Joe Gerard III, a baby Blaze kidnaps at the prompting of the voice of his dead partner in crime, George Rockley. Although Rockley is dead, his spirit is recreated in Blaze's mind to ease Blaze's utter isolation and feelings of loneliness that occur once his only friend is deceased. Blaze kidnaps the baby with the intent of ransoming it, but soon falls in love with it in a way that no rational adult could:

The dawning of the child's possibilities stole over him anew, and he shivered with the urge to snatch it up and cradle it to himself, to see Joe open his eyes and goggle around with his usual expression of perpetual wonder. With no knowledge of Wordsworth or Rousseau, he grasped the essential attraction infants have for adults; their cleanliness, their blankness, their portentious idiocy. And with Blaze, this feeling existed in a pureness that is rarely common to parents. He was not bright enough or motivated enough to have ambitions for the child or to want to mould its direction. Like a naturalist with a new species of plant, he wanted only to watch it grow. (141)

The story of Blaze is a prime indication of what King is trying to tell his readers: that it is important to synthesize child and adult perspectives. For while Blaze is a lovable character in his grownup state of innocence who can appreciate life in the way only a child can, it is his ignorance of adult behavior that culminates in his demise. His constant slip-ups, typical of inexperienced individuals, lead the law directly to him, and he is shot down in the woods where he has taken refuge with the baby. Blaze is merely an example of one extreme: the individual who can recall and perceive life through a child's eyes, and the one who avoids taking life too seriously. Yet, as has been explained, because Blaze cannot blend child experiences with adult experiences, he remains a helpless victim of a hostile world.

By thoroughly exploring the significance of youth in the chain of human development, King has succeeded in both continuing the theme as presented by his literary predecessors and commenting on the condition of young people in America. The concern for childhood and rites of passage can be linked directly to those American writers who made it a significant part of their fiction: Mark Twain, William Faulkner, Sherwood Anderson, Willa Cather, Flannery O'Connor, Joyce Carol Oates. The themes that pervade stories such as Twain's *Huckleberry Finn*, Oates' "Where Are You Going? Where Have You

Been?", and Faulkner's "Barn Burning" are the same ones that have had a profound influence on King's writing. Twain's Huck Finn embarks on a journey down the Mississippi River where his childhood innocence is constantly threatened by the adult world; likewise, King's Jack Sawyer in *The Talisman* ventures west across the expanse of America, a physical journey that correlates his evolution from innocence to experience. Oates' protagonist, Connie, is escorted away by evil incarnate, Arnold Friend, when she selfishly alienates herself and succumbs to wordly desires; King's Arnie Cunnigham in *Christine* makes a similar departure after isolating himself from society while searching for an identity. Faulkner's Sarty comes of age when he turns in his father for having burned a neighbor's farm after Sarty had repressed the truth of his father's evil acts for many years; in a similar situation, King's Danny Torrance (*The Shining*) confronts his father after deciding he is too enveloped in his own selfishly evil impulses to save himself. While these may be crude synopses, the themes concerning youth that King explores with such careful detail are the same that have helped earn his literary predecessors their greatness.

Because King is able to present an image of youth that is both optimistic and sympathetic, he provides a meaningful counterpoint to the tendencies of the American media to stereotype youth as troublesome. In a modernized America where young people are regularly exposed to input that consistently threatens to corrupt their innocence, King's portrayal of youth should be hailed as nothing less than splendid. By writing about youth as a time to be cherished, King assures his readers that they are not too far away from avoiding the self-destruction that can arise from failing to grasp the memories and lessons of being young. Closer scrutiny of King's fiction should convince readers that youth need not be observed as a strenuous period of development but rather one of significant meaning; by returning to younger days and rejoicing in their wonders and steps toward growth from a mature perspective, Americans can save themselves from being devoured by the moral, social, and economic pressures that so often dilute the magic of the human experience with age.

The material covered thus far does not do King proper justice. If one were to accumulate an adequate amount of critical interpretation on the political, social, and moral subtexts of King's works, one would easily fill up rows of library shelves much like those that are weighted with critical interpretations on Faulkner and Shakespeare.

The material discussed up to this point is an attempt to provide the reader with the knowledge that King is not just an entertainer—that there is more to acquire from a Stephen King book than just scares and thrills. As the ensuing sections aim to prove, King does not limit himself to any one area but rather attempts to address all spectres of the human condition in his canon, a feat that lesser writers of today's popular culture have been unable to achieve.

III. Technology: America's Sweetheart

An advanced technology has been the foundation of twentieth-century American superiority. Technological discoveries have not only led to fortune, they have led to a higher standard of living and increase in the well-being and comfort of humanity. But even more so, an advanced technology has fulfilled an American dream: to accomplish the most amount of work with the least amount of effort. Imagine what modern American society would be like without the benefit of microwave ovens, moving sidewalks, snowblowers, automobiles, remote controls, garage-door openers, automatic cash machines—all items so familiar to the American mind that they are often taken for granted. Stephen King seems to understand this higher American technology that often leaves its recipients salivating for an easier life. Through this recognition, King often suggests in his fiction that in their quest for devices to lessen the effort of any task, Americans have become literal slaves to their machines. King's awareness of this supplication to technology in America has caused him to pluck the real-life horrors stemming from technology and illustrate them in his fiction, something Douglas Winter adequately summarizes when observing the essential link between scientific advance and horror fiction in *Stephen King: The Art of Darkness*:

Our belated awareness of the negative implications of technology, coupled with growing doubts about the ability of technology to solve the complex problems of modern society, has rendered "technohorror" a theme of undeniable currency, requiring the horror writer to take but a simple step beyond front-page news. (98)

In effect, what King's fiction tends to show is that technology has indeed become America's seductive sweetheart, creating a dependency so profound and recurrent that Americans seldom realize they are subordinating themselves, compromising their humanity, in favor of technology's promises of ease.

The concept of a technology that reduces its creators to slobbering supplicants can be found throughout King's canon. No better example employing King's fundamental understanding of the subject can be found than in the short story "Trucks" (*Night Shift*). "Trucks" creates a scenario in which a group of individuals are trapped inside a roadside diner being encircled by packs of semi-trucks that have come alive, operating themselves without people behind their wheels. As the story continues, the trucks begin to panic when they realize they are running low on fuel. The people in the diner begin to understand that what the trucks really want out of them is constant refuelling; that if they appease the trucks by keeping their lifeblood flowing, the trucks will allow them to live. The narrator of the story acknowledges the true horror dawning before humanity when he comes upon the realization that the trucks need nothing but gas and periodic maintenance to survive; they do not need food, love, money, or anything else that characterizes their creators' humanness. The trucks, once created to serve humankind, are now emotionless heaps of metal without compassion, wanting absolutely nothing but the sustenance required to keep them running forever. This awareness of the trucks' simple, monotonous demands causes the narrator to identify the tedious doom facing humanity's future:

There were blisters in the soft webbing between thumb and index finger. But they wouldn't know about that. They would know about leaky manifolds and bad gaskets and frozen universal joints, but not about blisters or sun-stroke or the need to scream. They needed to know only one thing about their late masters, and they knew it. We bleed. (202)

Just as Victor Frankenstein's belief that his discovery of reanimating dead tissue into life seemed such an exciting breakthrough that the idea of meeting his creation's needs did not ever occur to him, so do Americans, whose quest for technological advance created the machines encircling the diner, fail to realize what their mechanical babies will someday require of them. Like Frankenstein and his monster, the people who gave birth to a device (automobiles) in the name of higher technology ultimately spawn an entity that runs their lives like a god: "A heavy hose dropped out of the rear like the umbilicus of some huge and dreadful god about to be born" (203).

There are several people in the diner who dissent from the idea of becoming servants to their own creations—"You want to be their living slaves?" the counterman had said. "That's what it'll come to. You want to spend the rest of your life changin' oil filters every time one of those things blasts its horn?" (204)—and try to escape, only to be run down by the metal machines awaiting them. The narrator even contemplates escape but stumbles upon the realization that turning away from technological advance would be tantamount to turning back the hands of time:

> We could run maybe. It would be easy to make the drainage ditch now, the way they're stacked up. Run through the fields, through the marshy places where trucks would bog down like mastadons and go—back to the caves.
>
> Drawing pictures in charcoal. This is the moon god. This is a tree. This is a Mack semi overwhelming a hunter. (204)

In the end, the survivors at the diner are left with nothing but a gas hose and a line of semis waiting for refuelling stretching as far as the eye can see. The seduction is complete: humans have created something thinking they can control it only to have the tables turned. The survivors have no hope of reversing the situation because to do so would be to give up on all that they have worked for in the twentieth century. Like modern Americans who labor endlessly maintaining their vehicles to assure that the machines continue to work for them, making their lives easier, the people in the diner must recognize the humbling truth that they must take responsibility for the mechanical children their desire for ease conceived.

"Trucks" is only one of King's stories using man-made mechanisms as appropriate vehicles for evil manifestations and supernatural phenomena. Two other short stories, "The Mangler" (*Night Shift*) and "Word Processor of the Gods" (*Skeleton Crew*) also employ the manipulation of human beings by their own technology created to serve them. "The Mangler" concerns a Hadley-Watson Model-6 Speed Ironer and Folder at an industrial laundromat that has been possessed by an evil spirit that traps the limbs of its operators (the subject material for this story was most likely inspired by King's working at an industrial laundromat to help in paying bills before he became a full-time writer). Once the operators are trapped, the machine 'mangles' its victims. When two men try to exorcize the spirit from the machine, it tears itself from its bolts and becomes a walking, stalking beast preying on humanity. Like "The Mangler," "The Word Processor of the Gods" depicts humans being victimized by a man-made mechanism manufactured to lessen humans' workloads. The story is of a word processor left to a man by his dead nephew that allows him to make or unmake reality by simply typing a word or phrase and then hitting the RETURN or DELETE keys. The man can change the entire course of his family's lives, such as making his wife thin where before she had been grossly overweight. He can wipe out his wife and son in exchange for his nephew and sister-in-law, who he believed had been wrongfully matched with his wicked, self-serving brother, who killed the two in a drunk-driving accident.

While he depicts an America victimized by its technology, King also implies that American society is in its own peculiar way married to its mechanisms. In the novel *Christine*, King attempts to show that men are so attached to their machines that they often use pronouns such as 'she' and 'her'—human labels—when describing them; machines in this sense take on human connotations. In the case of Christine, Arnie Cunnigham is 'married' to his car; the man-made mechanism becomes his surrogate lover. The book's title should give an immediate implication of Arnie's relationship to the '57 Plymouth Fury; the title implies a human being, a female, but the book is not about a woman but rather a car. Arnie treats his car like he would treat his heart's love: he caresses her; he fondles her; he tends to her like a nurturing relative when she is not running correctly. He devotes all of his spare time to restoring the car after purchasing it in a decrepit condition. King even uses sexual imagery to describe Arnie's trying to push Christine after she has been damaged by Arnie's enemies:

He had put Christine's transmission in neutral and pushed her, pushed her until she began to roll on her flat tires, pushed her until she was out the door and he could hear the wind of November keening sharply around the wrecks and the abandoned hulks with their stellated glass and their ruptured gas tanks; he had pushed her until the sweat ran off him in rivers and his heart thudded like a runaway horse in his chest and his back cried out for mercy; he had pushed her, his body pumping as if in some hellish consummation; he had pushed her, and inside the odometer ran backward, and some fifty feet beyond the door his back began to really throb, and he kept pushing, and then his back began to scream in protest, and he kept pushing, muscling it along the flat, slashed tires, his hands going numb, his back screaming, screaming, screaming. (334-35)

In the following passage, Arnie has a vision in which he and Christine are united in holy matrimony:

Suddenly something very like a vision rose in his tired, confused mind. He was hearing a minister's voice: Arnold, do you take this woman to be your loving—

But it wasn't a church; it was a used-car lot with bright multicolored plastic pennants fluttering in a stiff breeze. Camp chairs had been set up. It was Will Darnell's lot, and Will was standing beside him in the best man's position. There was no girl beside him. Christine was parked beside him, shining in a spring sun, even her whitewalls seeming to glow.

His father's voice: Is there something going on?

The preacher's voice: Who giveth this man to this woman?

Roland D. LeBay rose from one of the camp chairs like the prow of a skeletal ghost-ship from Hades. He was grinning—and for the first time Arnie saw who had been sitting around him: Buddy Repperton, Richie Trelawney, Moochie Welch [all people who'd been killed by Christine]. Richie Trelawney was black and charred, most of his hair burned off. Blood had poured down Buddy Repperton's chin and had caked his shirt like hideous vomit. But Moochie Welch was the worst; Moochie Welch had been ripped open like a laundry bag. They were smiling. All of them were smiling.

I do, Roland D. LeBay croaked. He grinned, and a tongue slimed with graveyard mould lolled from the stinking hole of his mouth. I give her, and he's got the receipt to prove it. She's all his. The bitch is the ace of spades...and she's all his. (331-32)

Arnie becomes so attached to his car that he ultimately alienates himself from humanity. The car becomes all the "significant other" that he could ever need, which is a situation that ends up in disaster. As the story illustrates, Americans' subordination of their humanness in favor of surrounding themselves in technology's immediate gratifications leads to their demise.

Yet while King succeeds in painting a grim portrait of the relationship between Americans and their technology, he also seems to be aware that modern science has made significant advances in furthering the human race. A story like "The Woman in the Room" (*Night Shift*) suggests that King recognizes modern medical science has found methods to cure and console the ill. King is not ignorant of the benefits of modern technology; what he is concerned with is human ignorance of both its limitations and its potentials. Examine the following scene from the story in which the protagonist is visiting the hospital where his mother, who has cancer, is wasting away:

There are pieces of hospital equipment here and there, like strange playground toys. A litter with a clear white sheet on it, the kind they use to wheel you up to the "O.R." where they take out your gall bladder or put plastic tubes in your heart or give you a "cortotomy" or any number of other operations. There is a large circular object whose function is unknown to him. It is made of stainless steel pipes and looks like a double ferris wheel. There is a rolling IV tray with two bottles hung from it like transparent teats. (400)

This passage suggests the protagonist's alienation from modern science in its fruitless efforts to control the processes of terminal disease and natural death. The story argues that people utilize technology to its extreme while remaining ignorant to the fact that there are simply some things beyond human control. In the story's end, heedless of the numerous instruments and machines trying to combat his mother's illness, only the protagonist knows how to ease her suffering and set her free—he commits matricide.

When King is writing about technology, tragedy often results from humans' overanticipation of conquering the unknown for the sake of advancing technology. *The Mist*, a novella in *Skeleton Crew*, is the story of a town's capture by prehistoric monsters unleashed by a secret governmental experiment known as the Arrowhead Project. *The Stand* is the story of the massive reduction of the American population due to an escaped flu virus being researched by the U.S. government for germ warfare. At the end of the novel, a portion of the remaining humans are wiped out by another symbol of American technological ignorance, the nuclear bomb. "The Jaunt" (*Skeleton Crew*) concerns the breakthrough discovery of being able to transport objects over vast stretches of space by transporting their atoms, much like the crew of the Starship Enterprise did when one yelled "Beam me up, Scottie!" What a man and his family find out is that there are things existing beyond the three-dimensional world as humans know it that cannot be understood. After making a 'jaunt' with his family from Earth to Mars, the man is given a rude awakening to the dark side of technological advance when his son arrives behind him a white-haired, jibbering fool. What the son had seen in the dimension he entered while 'jaunting' was so indescribable that it made him insane.

What King calls to attention recurringly in his fiction is that American technology has run away with itself. It has made a slave of the master, it has taken the place of humanity in its ability to alienate humans from their fellows, and it has created a momentum that humans cannot control just as they could not slow a runaway freight train. King's fiction stimulates the American intellect into questioning the implications of living in an advanced technological state, and it continuously asks that Americans be keen in their skepticism concerning who made who. Unless humanity can keep its machines and inventions in perspective and understand their potentials, the creations conceived to aid humans will destroy them and keep them in perpetual bondage. By illustrating these outcomes, King consistently shines a spotlight on the American public that remains ignorant of the horrifying realities of uncontrolled scientific advance, the public that chooses rather to solicit the promises of ease offered by its sweetheart, technology.

IV. Caught in the Machine of American Capitalism

Being himself an American who has achieved the American dreams of wealth and fame, Stephen King has often directed his attention toward what it means to be an American in search of the ultimate goals of riches and recognition. A close reading of the economic commentary in King's fiction often reveals that he is more concerned with the spiritual corruption capitalism breeds than the promises of luxury resulting from material gain. When King is dealing with Americans in pursuit of profit and power in his stories, he often highlights the negative consequences and attitudes arising from the selfish interpretations of capitalist ideologies.

A working definition of capitalism, central to this discussion, can be found in *The American Heritage Dictionary*: "an economic system, characterized by a free market and open competition, in which goods are produced for profit, labor is performed for wages, and the means of production and distribution are privately owned." While it may seem silly to reiterate a concept well understood by the American public, one must also realize that most Americans probably have only a generalized understanding of capitalism and do not read the words defining it closely enough to understand what they actually emphasize. Close attention to phrases used to define—free market, open competition, privately owned—soon reveals that the capitalist ideology in itself promotes a war among neighbors in its emphasis on the self before the community. Unlike communism or socialism, which both steer toward spreading wealth among the community, reducing the number of wealthy figureheads as compared to America, American capitalism reinforces isolation and deception as imperative in order to assure furthering the self toward capital gain. Because capitalism supports competition in an open market, people will naturally alienate themselves from others in competing for their personal goals.

Also central to an understanding of capitalist ideology when discussing King's fiction is its direct relationship with moral choice. Often in King's stories, people are faced with the moral choice of whether to selfishly appease the self in acquiring personal gain regardless of the consequences or to surrender that gain for the sake of righteousness and the well-being of others. This link between America's economic ideology and moral choice arises directly from the paradox created by the coexistence of capitalism and America's predominant religion, Christianity. The two ideologies simply oppose each other. The New Testament preaches that people should love their neighbors, that they should share with others, that they must help those in need, that they store their treasures in heaven rather than on earth. These concepts do not coincide with those of open competition, free market, and private ownership, where the emphasis is not on sharing and keeping wealth in heaven but rather is on making as much gain as possible, preferably more than one's neighbor. Simply put, how can people strive to better themselves and establish their material greatness yet humble themselves and act selflessly at the same time? Companies such as IBM, Coca-Cola, and Chrysler would not likely have found favorable mention in the books of Matthew, Mark, Luke, or John.

The sad conclusion to this paradox, reinforced strongly by American media, is that the desire for personal material wealth often exceeds the need to participate in a working, meaningful society based on loving, caring, sharing, and friendship. One does not need to look far in the media to gain an understanding of the strong emphasis placed on achieving fame and glory: *MTV, Entertainment Tonight, Hard Copy, Lifestyles of the Rich and Famous*. By consistently exposing themselves to the lives of luxury being realized by people such as Michael Jackson, Madonna, Elizabeth Taylor, M.C. Hammer, Ted Turner, and Donald Trump, Americans continue to want more, more, more. In effect, whatever material possessions Americans do have, it is not enough, resulting in the notion of material gain as the major focal point of American society, a focal point that breeds jealousy, envy, greed, and alienation.

King gives evidence in his non-fiction that he is skeptical toward capitalism in the greed and selfishness it has embedded in the American mind. In "Culch" and "Your Kind of Place," two unpublished essays stored at the Raymond H. Fogler Special Collections Department at UMO, King talks about the American addiction to material goods and the McDonald's Corporation as a model for the American dream of wealth and power. In "Culch," King recalls his mother's word for junk, a word she applied to all the meaningless goods and products Americans become so attached to:

The point to make about my mother is that, enthusiastic as she was, she was also a New Englander, a Mainer to be even more specific, and she recognized the fact that a young boy's course to manhood in America is lined and heaped with all the things that made Pinocchio's nose grow long...she understood the attraction of culch, its necessity, even...the great understanding she brought to that wonderful, condemnatory word was this: If culch is to be recognized, if its worst manifestations are to be avoided, immunization is necessary. Especially in America, the world's citadel of culch. (3)

The item of "culch" King refers to in the essay is an x-ray machine at a local shoe store where his mother had bought him a pair of Buster Browns. By slipping a coin into the machine, patrons could see an x-ray of their feet. The young Stephen became infatuated with the machine, supporting his mother's notion that Americans are trained dogs who salivate over anything new and inventive, despite its apparent lack of meaning or usefulness. What King argues is that although the machine had no true contribution to his humanity, he was still one of the many who was willing to pop the coin in the slot for its useless gratification.

"Your Kind of Place" augments King's perception of the effects of capitalism on the American mind by describing the rise to power of Ray Kroc, who built the *McDonald*'s fast-food chain empire. The essay uses Kroc as a model because his rise was the realization of every American's dream. Kroc started out selling milkshake mixers in Illinois. Then he heard of a small food chain operation in southern California run by two brothers with the surname *MacDonald*. Kroc smelled opportunity, and he began to formulate ideas about the potential of such an industry—an industry where a person could walk in, place an order, and receive it in minutes without the formalities of most walk-in restaurants. Kroc then flew out to introduce his ideas to the MacDonald brothers, who, after hearing them, liked his ideas and let him into the operation. Kroc's innovative schemes to build the food chain from a few stores to a multitude were successful. Soon, Kroc was chief shareholder of the business. He bumped out the MacDonald brothers and took the reigns. When the MacDonald brothers opened their own burger joint across the street from one of Kroc's, Kroc filed suit and forced them to close. King was interested in this scenario because it is filled with all the implications of American capitalism:

There is a certain texture to American success—it's something that is more than the five senses, but a part of them. The big Camels billboard in

Manhattan, the one that used to blow smoke-rings from the girl's mouth, had it. The Ford assembly line had it. Certain movie screen faces have it. It is a felt thing, a mental texture, nearly erotic to a certain kind of American brain. It is sensed, and that brain comes fully alert and aware, trembling delicately. Financial awareness is suffused with blood and comes erect. (1)

King also uses McDonald's as an adequate model of capitalism in that it successfully seduces and brainwashes the public into admiring its grandiosity. As King points out in the essay, "According to a company survey, 96% of American children can identify Ronald McDonald. He is topped only by Santa Claus. My own children, who are four and two, are not sure of Jesus, but they understand Ronald perfectly" (3). By illustrating both the rise to power of Ray Kroc and the accompanying influence of his empire over the American public, King's rendition of the McDonald's saga highlights a number of vices often pervading American fiction: greed, alienation, and manipulation.

The feelings King expresses in "Culch" and "Your Kind of Place" often appear in his fiction. One of the loudest statements concerning the misgivings of capitalism in his stories can be found in the short story "Graveyard Shift" (*Night Shift*). The story takes place in a decrepit rural Maine textile mill overrun by a population of rats. The mill is run by a man named Warwick, who represents a selfish capitalist concerned with reaping the profits of the industry with no regard for anyone but himself. He is in a postion of power because his employees are all dependent on the small amount of income received from the job. Because of their dependency they are forced to work ludicrous hours in hazardous conditions. When Warwick suspects a visit from the health inspector, he gathers a group of workers to clean the mill's wasteland of a basement. While cleaning the basement and flushing the rats out to the stream outside, Warwick and a few employees uncover a trap door leading underground. Inspection of the subterranean cavern reveals a group of mutant rats that have been breeding there for years. The protagonist, Hall, soon comes to realize that it was the carelessness of the ownership in alienating itself from humanity and the mill in sole pursuit of personal profit that allowed these atrocities to breed:

Something had happened to the rats back here, some hideous mutation that never could have survived under the eye of the sun; nature would have forbidden it. But down here, nature had taken on another ghastly face. (76)

The mutant rats would never have been conceived under nature's natural laws, but with the aid of human avarice born of a selfish interpretation of capitalistic ideology, they find a welcome birthplace in the underground of the textile mill.

King continues his image of an American society swallowing itself in pursuit of selfish goals in his novel *Needful Things*. The novel concerns the deterioration of a small town after an entrepreneur, Leland Gaunt, opens a shop with a rather curious inventory: he sells those goods that he knows most appeal to each of the town's individual residents. After discovering that Gaunt has the things they most desire, the people of Castle Rock are willing to pay any price to obtain them. Gaunt capitalizes on American attitudes such as those exemplified by Castle Rockian Brian Rusk, who sells his humanity to purchase a rare Sandy Koufax baseball card:

...he found that he now wanted the Sandy Koufax card more than ever. He had discovered another large fact about possessions and the peculiar psychological state they induce: the more one has to go through because of something one owns, the more he wants to keep that thing. (245)

While Brian's initial interest in the card was simple want, his preoccupation with the card is intensified after executing Gaunt's demand in exchange for it: he must play a trick on another Castle Rockian, a trick that triggers a hate war between two women who had previously disliked each other. The prank is physically and emotionally demanding of Brian, whose desire to covet the card is strengthened by his realization of its price. Brian's fall from humanity correlates with the American tendency to pursue material gain ruthlessly, a pursuit that exponentially magnifies the end goal.

King also illustrates through *Needful Things* that nothing comes for free; in order for Americans to have the possessions they want, they must be willing to pay the price. As Gaunt so aptly explains to Myra Evans, who had acquired a picture of Elvis Presley that magically produces a euphoric fantasy in which Myra is intimate with "The King," she cannot simply have the picture to herself without fulfilling her contract for it:

"...You promised, and you're going to make good on your promise. You'll be very sorry if you don't, Myra."

She had heard a brittle cracking. She looked down and saw with horror that a jagged crack now split the glass over The King's face.

"No!" she cried. "No, don't do that!"

"I'm not doing it," Mr. Gaunt had responded with a laugh. "You're doing it. You're doing it by being a silly, lazy little cunt. This is America, Myra, where only whores do business in bed. In America respectable people have to get out of bed and earn the things they need, or lose them forever. I think you forgot that." (419)

Gaunt possesses the essential understanding that Americans have a need for things, and that they must work and compromise themselves to have their things. In the case of Myra, she, like Brian Rusk, must play a catastrophic prank in order to finish her business with Gaunt, a prank she must carry out if she wishes to keep the one thing she truly wants.

Another vivid example of capitalism's manipulation of American minds in its corruption of their spirits appears in *The Shining*. The tragedy of the novel lies in protagonist Jack Torrance's alienation from his family in favor of the long list of gratuities offered by the supernatural inhabitants of the Overlook Hotel, where Torrance has taken his family to maintain the hotel during the winter season. Jack, a school teacher in between jobs who is struggling with his writing career, has his expectations as an American male placed in jeopardy after being fired from his last job for striking a student. He faces all the humiliations so feared by American males, who are conditioned into assuming that they must assert themselves through success in all trades; his career stands on shaky ground, he is not steadily employed, and he is barely supporting his family. The Overlook ultimately becomes attractive to Jack because it promises to provide him with a new sense of machismo. Through establishing a bond with the Overlook, Jack once again feels powerful: with no one else but his family surrounding him in the vastness of the hotel, Jack is given a feeling of superiority and control of his life. Because the Overlook is keen to Jack's despair, it seduces him and capitalizes on his need for confidence; the price Jack must pay for the Overlook's promises demands that he alienate himself from his family so that he can concentrate on his own concerns of self-promotion. As Burton Hatlen suggests, "Indeed, within the novel the Overlook comes to represent a broad American social and historical context which both contributes to and reflects the tragedy of the Torrance family" (99). In tune with capitalist ideology, Jack is willing to sacrifice all in his pursuit to better himself.

The Overlook is indeed the embodiment of the capitalist society surrounding it: it derives its power from the suffering and expendability of others, a characteristic of which Jack becomes a contributor in his pursuit of self-promotion, much as any major American corporation may dehumanize people with the sole intent of making the corporation more prominent. The Overlook is not concerned with morality, spirituality, or human bonding but rather is solely concerned with corrupting Jack and reaping the benefits of his breach of humanity, a flaw that is a vital ingredient to the augmentation of the hotel's supernatural powers. If one pays attention to the Overlook's history as explained in the novel, one will find that its significant late inhabitants, most notably the wealthy entrepreneur Horace Derwent, were individuals who had staked their fortunes on the losses of their humanity in the tradition of Jay Gatsby. By selfishly stealing the souls of its inhabitants in exchange for promises of grandeur, the Overlook is able to accumulate a dynamo of power bred of human corruption. Hatlen aptly concludes the Overlook's part in King's scheme of defining the curses of capitalism, arguing that:

he [Jack] also learns how the rich control the world, and he is forced to recognize that their money is finally more important to them than their friends. Not only the family but the social order as a whole has, then, a structure which shapes what happens to people; and in *The Shining* the hotel represents the macrostructure of an exploitative society within which the small tragedy of the Torrance family inexorably works itself out. (100)

Since capitalism is based on free-market, open competition, every person is left on his or her own in the pursuit of capital gain. Because of this individual-based characteristic, not everyone has an equal amount of access to the means of production and wealth. Since America is fundamentally a male-dominated society, the majority of the country's wealth is handled or is believed to be handled by its middle- and upper-class white male population. This concentration breeds certain attitudes and stereotypes, producing images of white male power and minority weakness. Those males controlling the bulk of wealth dictate to the country's males that white men have an access to superiority not available to their minority peers, culminating in a tendency to subordinate the remaining population: children, blacks, Hispanics, the elderly. This subordination is reinforced by American media, which depicts white males as holding the reigns of power while their weaker female, black, child, and elderly counterparts are the frail followers stirring in their wake. Seldom are these latters portrayed in the media as capable of equalling the supreme, powerful, domineering personalities found in white males—Rambo, James Bond, Indiana Jones, Dirty Harry, Blake Carrington (*Dynasty*). Stephen King is also guilty of failing to create strong, autonomous minority characters in his fiction, a fault that even when consciously acknowledged still causes him problems. Critic Chelsea Quinn Yarbro had this to say about America's most successful author:

It is disheartening when a writer with so much talent and strength and vision is not able to develop a believable woman character between the ages of seventeen and sixty. (49)

King admitted that even when he tries to develop an autonomous female character, she often evolves into a she-devil. This supports some white American male perceptions of women as threatening and unstable. Several of King's leading female characters—Carrie White, Annie Wilkes (*Misery*), Ardelia Lortz (*The Library Policeman*), and Wendy Torrance (*The Shining*)—which are indeed few, are either vehicles of destruction (Carrie, Annie, and Ardelia) or subject to the shortcomings of their male peers (Wendy). This attitude arising from a white, male-dominated capitalist economy is something King has increasingly become aware of. It is illustrated by King's response to Yarbro's criticism of him, taken from his interview with *Playboy* magazine:

PLAYBOY: Along with your difficulty in describing sexual scenes, you apparently also have a problem with women in your books. Critic Chelsea Quinn Yarbro wrote, [check above quote]. Is this a fair criticism?

KING: Yes, unfortunately, I think it is probably the most justifiable of all those levelled at me. In fact, I'd extend her criticism to include my handling of black characters. Both Hallorrann, the cook in *The Shining*, and Mother Abigail in *The Stand* are cardboard caricatures of superblack heroes, viewed through rose-tinted glasses of white liberal guilt. And when I think I'm free of that charge that most male American writers depict women as either nebbishes or bitch-goddess destroyers, I create someone like Carrie—who starts out as a nebbish victim and then becomes a bitch goddess, destroying an entire town in an explosion of hormonal rage. I recognize the problems but can't yet rectify them. (BB 47)

It is quite likely that this self-criticism inevitably led to the writing of *Gerald's Game* and *Dolores Claiborne*, which both depict women standing up against a world that tries to reduce their status as human beings. Neither portrays its leading women as "nebbishes" or "bitch-goddess destroyers" but rather as assertive, autonomous individuals with the strength to survive.

In an attempt to oppose the attitudes stemming from an image of white male superiority, King has in the past gone so far as to create such a detestable character as Lester Billings ("The Boogeyman"). The story provides a sardonic portrayal of the typical male product of American society. Billings had to drop out of college some time ago to work loading Pepsi machines to support his family, which he had started much too young. Yet while Billings comes across as an egocentric failure, he maintains his conviction that he is indeed superior in his maleness and clings to his machismo. The following scene takes place in Billing's psychiatrist's office (another parody on Billing's ego, for while Billings thinks he has all the answers, he still needs professional help), where Billings is relaying the horrors unravelling at his home where a monster has been hiding in his closet and murdering his children. His wife had suggested bringing their daughter into their room after their first son was killed in his, where Billings had demanded he be left before he was murdered:

"I wanted to take her into our room for the night."
"Did you?"
"…no." Billings regarded his hands, and his face twitched painfully. "How could I go to Rita, admit I was wrong? I had to be strong. She was always such a jellyfish…look how easy she went to bed with me when we weren't married." Harper said: "On the other hand, look how easily you went to bed with her." Billings froze in the act of rearranging his hands, and slowly turned his head to look at Harper. "Are you trying to be a wise guy?"
"No, indeed," Harper said.
"Then let me tell it my way," Billings snapped. "I'm not going to talk about my sex life, if that's what you expect. Rita and I had a very normal sex life, with none of that dirty stuff. I know it gives some people a charge to talk about that, but I'm not one of them." (3-4)

Billings adheres so strongly to his image of white machismo that he cannot admit any notion of sensitivity. Trapped inside his ego, he feels impelled to internalize his feelings and to refrain from sharing himself with others. In effect, the gross exaggeration of Billing's self-image deserves humor although his superfluous arrogance results in tragedy.

At the same time King is able to satirize the occasional absurdity of American maleness, he is humble enough to criticize himself and his profession as being worthy of satire in the capitalist scene. King recognizes that he is living a child's dream—that he is paid large sums of money for writing stories while millions of others engage in more tedious work for much lesser wages. He is not so proud of what he does that he cannot poke fun at the concept of being a millionaire writer, something he does at certain points in *Secret Window, Secret Garden*, a novella in *Four Past Midnight*. The story is about a best-selling author named Mort Rainey, who has been accused of plagiarism by a Mississippi man named John Shooter. He is a writer and he claims that Rainey has published a story almost straight from one of Shooter's own manuscripts. When Rainey reflects on whether or not Shooter is telling the truth about his profession, he begins to see characteristics in Shooter that might support his claim:

Maybe Shooter was a writer. He fulfilled both of the main requirements: he told a tale you wanted to hear to the end, even if you had a pretty good idea what the end was going to be, and he was so full of shit he squeaked. (281)

While King can poke fun at his profession, he also dives into the dark side of being a successful figurehead in a capitalist society. In America, those who have achieved wealth and fame are catapulted into the realm of celebrity. Along with this celebrity status can come the feeling of being alienated or separated from the commonfolk, a group that King respects. One can find without much difficulty that a large number of King's stories are about successful writers, and, after reading those stories, one may begin to assume that King is saying fame and glory have a profound dark half. The extent to which the stories are autobiographical is not fully known; however, simply reading them gives good indications concerning King's feelings about achieving the American dream of success. No better example can be found than in *Misery*, a novel about a popular writer's captivity inside the home of a mentally disturbed, overzealous fan who forces him to revive a character he'd put to rest. The following passage from *Secret Window, Secret Garden* also helps in illustrating the plight of the popular American writer in Mort Rainey's description of his wife's feelings about his celebrity status:

His success at his chosen trade after the years of struggle had been a great and fulfilling thing for him; he sometimes felt like a man who has won his way through a perilous jungle where most other adventurers perish and has gained a fabulous prize by so doing. Amy had been glad for him, at least initially, but for her there had been a bitter downside: the loss of her identity not only as a private person but as a separate person. (296)

Expressed feelings such as these in his fiction support King's recognition of the paradox of achieving the ultimate goals of the American capitalistic dream at the expense of losing the self.

King also attempts to overcome the attitudes arising from the American hunger for luxurious lifestyles by including a large number of common people as his main protagonists. Much of today's popular culture entertainment tends to reinforce capitalist goals by centering on the rich and famous, intensifying the common masses' desire to achieve that status. Because the main characters in Jackie Collins, Danielle Steele, and Sidney Sheldon novels are often the wealthy and powerful, they distort the public's view of themselves. While the public reads to escape into a world of glamour, they are also humbling themselves by affirming that there are those who have what they cannot have. The stories produced by these writers tend to firmly support the notions of capitalism: that material gain is the ultimate goal, that people deceive others for their own selfish needs, that the rich are immoral, and that the rich are content with their immorality because they are rich. What separates King from his contemporaries is that he creates a breach in this American vision by departing from characters who are the manifestation of the American capitalist dream and centering more on commonfolk, who realistically constitute the bulk of America's population. By focusing on common individuals, King restores the truth that the rich and famous are the exception and not the rule.

While people in America live in perpetual envy of the affluent, King attempts to remind his readers that each American's life is significant in its contribution to the American system, and that each American's life is unique and worthy of discussion in any body of fiction. In fact, one may reasonably argue that common individuals are even more worthy of inclusion in fiction because those people who do not have the advantages of money and power in combatting adversity must often summon the raw courage within themselves to avoid succumbing to their world. As Samuel Schuman points out in the following passage, the common, publically unidentifiable individual is often the most useful in writing horror fiction:

For "fright fiction" to work most effectively, it must focus upon a rather particular sort of character. The horror writer's protagonists must be sufficiently virtuous to win our sympathy, but sufficiently imperfect to seem recognizably human. They must be on the one hand interesting and unique, and on the other, "normal" and typical—otherwise, the evils which beset them will not be fully frightening to a readership which is, by and large, normal and typical. King's characters adhere exactly to these specifications. They are overwhelmingly middle-class, protestant, white, Americans. They are interested in earning a comfortable living. They are dutiful fathers, mothers, and children. They will err occasionally, but their sins are not gigantic (although they can plunge them into enormous nightmares) and seem almost comfortably domestic. (112)

While his previously mentioned contemporaries are successful in churning out their tales of the trials and tribulations of the rich and powerful, it may well be that King exceeds them in sales because his stories have a subconscious appeal to his readers not inclusive in the others due in part to King's common characters. Perhaps King's readers enjoy his books because they can pick up one and likely find an individual with whom they can identify on a more realistic level instead of envy. After all, with a few exceptions, King's characters are often as common as the person next door: Arnie Cunnigham, Carrie White, Jack Torrance, Jack Sawyer, Mark Petrie, Kevin Delevan, Sheriff Alan Pangborn, The Loser's Club, Harold Lauder. These characters are not rich and famous, are not prodigies, and are not in positions of significant societal influence. Critic Deborah Notkin supports the appeal of King's common characters to his readers when she writes that:

there is hardly a novel of King's that does not make room for the ignored characters of literature—children, non- caucasians, the disabled. In *The Stand*, one of the heroes is deaf [Tom Cullen], not because it is necessary to the plot, but simply because some people are deaf and King is attempting to write about a cross-section of humanity. In an increasingly homogenized culture, any attempt to remind us that we leave a lot of people out of our picture of "people" can only be a good thing. (141)

While King recognizes his susceptibility to adhere to traditional white American male attitudes and the effects of American capitalist ideology, he attempts to overcome this tendency in a number of ways. Not only does he investigate these principles by highlighting the extremities of both distorted male self-images and the shortcomings of fame, he also increasingly labors to include minority characters who are self-efficient individuals in his fiction. These characters are best exemplified by Hallorrann, Mother Abigail, and Mike Hanlon (*It*)—all blacks—and characters such as Donna Trenton (*Cujo*), Bev Rogan (*It*), and Dolores Claiborne—all females. King has also attempted to make his children capable of asserting themselves against white male adult adversaries, something he has been able to accomplish with Danny Torrance, Mark Petrie (*'Salem's Lot*), The Loser's Club (*It*), Jack Sawyer (*The Talisman*), and Kevin Delevan (*The Sun Dog*). This increase in inclusion of strong minority characters makes King a significant extension of twentieth-century fiction; while his American literary predecessors were powerful in their renditions of the human condition, much of their subject material was centered around males. While King may suffer from criticism of not creating completely well-rounded minority characters, the simple fact that he has made the effort to do so while living under the shadow of white male domination in his wealthy, white, upper-class status should give a good indication of his concern for the human race.

V. Autonomy versus Societal Conformity in America

As this survey of American commentary in Stephen King's fiction has suggested, King has been successful in weaving a myriad of issues into his stories. While some of his stories focus more on one area than others, a close reading of his works will often show that King seldom fails to include a wide view of American society. One of the leading themes in his fiction is that of the plight of Americans caught between pursuing the American dreams of life, liberty, and individual happiness and surrendering those values for the sake of keeping the societal machine rolling. The preceding section on capitalism emphasized that America's economic system reinforces the notion of individual gain based on open competition, but the section also argued that people are often made expendable for the furtherance of a larger body. This tendency of American businesses to dehumanize people in a push for corporate greatness can be applied to a larger level when seen from the light that America, while highlighting the celebration of individuality, often contradicts itself by subordinating personal interests to societal expectations.

King often brings to light in his fiction that while Americans pursue meaningful lives individually, they are often expected to conform to some group order; that pressure to conform can come from a number of sources: family, community, the workplace, the government; all of these sources require a degree of individual compromise for a peaceful group existence. The failure to conform to larger groups because of personal beliefs can often lead to isolation and tension among peers. For example, Americans need only look to the media, where during the past several years an increasing wave of conflict has arisen over the interpretation of the First Amendment; those who are more free-spirited, such as pop singer Madonna, who blends sexuality and religion in her performances, tend to see the amendment as allowing a complete freedom of expression. Yet there still exists a large movement of conservatives adhering to a moral code that feels it necessary to censor the expressive freedom of its liberal counterparts. While conservatives may be able to recognize the validity of liberals' need to exercise their freedom of expression, they may also feel the need to restrain an open application of that freedom, seeing liberals as non-conformants to traditional values of purity and morality. This conflict of ideas can create a breach in communication between family members, employers and employees, and the government and its constituents, which may all result in a lack of social harmony.

Stephen King recognizes the powerful dilemma of deciding exactly where the line separating automony and societal conformity should be drawn. On the one hand, he sees the subordination of the self to higher powers as limiting and suppressing. Yet he also realizes that the human condition has a strong need for organization, which, when formulated without selfish intent, can be a source of significant bonding and brotherhood in support of good will. It is only when people become too dependent on larger groups that their autonomy is gradually weakened—a concept that King explores to argue that people need a balance between dependency on the self and societal organizations to avoid being completely swallowed by their worlds.

King's recognition of individuals' ambiguous roles in society was expressed before he was published as an author. When a college student at the University of Maine at Orono, King was politically active, not afraid to voice his opinions. In the April 16, 1970, "King's Garbage Truck," King articulated his dismay over an incident where he had been handing out leaflets for The Rally for Free Speech to be held in the Memorial Union at UMO. He had given a leaflet to an elderly lady, who accused him as being a "scummy radical bastard":

How did I become a scummy radical bastard? Well, I started out with the belief that America once was and should again be a country of individuals, a country where one isn't the loneliest number but the most important. This doesn't seem like a radical idea—it is the basis of the Declaration of Independence, the Constitution, and even the Articles of Confederation— but in 1970 it seems to make you a scummy radical bastard, all right.... Just suppose you accept the idea that, in a democratic nation, the individual is the most important item on the agenda. Think of the camp that puts you in!...It means you can't accept the draft, which legislates the freedom of choice into a murderous knee-jerk. It means that you must protest a war in which you look the way you feel like looking. It means that you use whatever stimulants amuse you be they beer, whiskey, pot, mescaline, LSD, morphine, or heroin. It means that you must read, live, and decide on all questions of morality without the benefit of B'Nai B'Rith, the Daughters of the American Revolution, the Catholic Church, the Minutemen, or—well,

you name it. In short, it means that you must participate in the decisions of
what is best for yourself and for your brothers—not hand them over to Big
Brother.... I'm reminded of that scene in *Easy Rider* when Jack Nicholson
looks at Peter Fonda and Dennis Hopper with a kind of puzzled
bewilderment and says: "You know, this used to be a hell of a good
country." Well, it did. It could be again. But not until we realize that the real
American way (if there ever was such a thing) is to think and feel for
yourself, not to leave it up to some juiceless fool in Washington.

This skepticism with which King observed the treatment of
individuality in America has spread far into his career as a best-selling
novelist. In fact, King's first three published novels, while dealing with
other issues, are all centered around the conflict bred of the
conformants and non-conformants of society. In *Carrie*, Carrie White
is pressured by her peers to surrender her autonomy in favor of
maintaining her lowly placement on the high-school social scale.
When Carrie refuses to conform to her peers' expectations of her to
remain weak and timid by revealing her femininity at the high school
prom, she is subjected to their cruelty. Like *Carrie*, *'Salem's Lot*,
while on the surface a novel about a town's assault by a league of
vampires, is concerned with the repression of autonomy by societal
expectations of conformity. Using the fictional town of Jerusalem's
Lot, King portrays a microcosm where a person's notions of
individuality are swallowed by the community. The people of
Jerusalem's Lot are much more concerned with the moral status of
their neighbors than their own. Whenever a 'Salem's Lot resident
appears to be involved in something of an eccentric nature, that rebel
is quickly made aware by peers that he or she has strayed from the
norm. King's description of this interaction between neighbors
suggests that the town is in itself a living, breathing entity larger than
the common individuals inhabiting it that needs for all of its organs to
be faithful to it. When one of its organs (an individual) does not
function properly, it needs to be corrected harshly. This tendency to
supress individuality results in the widespread alienation that allows
the destruction of the town to occur. As Douglas Winter writes of the
novel, "paradoxically, the city's man-made landscape is an obvious
symbol of our social and technological development, whose goal was
to supplant the chaos of nature with an ordered society" (AOD 42).
Both novels display the end result of an imbalance between
autonomy and social interaction: tragedy. In the novels, people are
forced to surrender themselves to societal expectations, allowing the
seeds of disaster to be sown.

King's third novel, *The Shining*, also depicts a conflict arising from the pressures and expectations of conformity to a larger group, yet it differs from the first two in that it mainly focuses on a smaller sect of society, the family. The tragedy that unwinds within the Torrance family rises directly from a combination of the family unit's inability to fulfill each member's expectations and the Torrances' realization that the family is threatening each of their personal interests. In times of stress, the Torrances cannot come together as a family unit; on the contrary, when one of the Torrances looks within the family for resolution, the family's failure to fulfill that need leads to individual isolation. Jack's failure to act responsibly in his role as father and husband leads to Wendy's alienation from him. Likewise, the marital discord between his parents leads Danny to separate himself from them. When Jack's expectations that his family understand his maintaining the hotel as a means for re-establishing his dependability as a responsible worker are not met, whatever feelings of fondness he has for them begin to dissipate rapidly. Even when Jack starts to realize that the hotel is having adverse effects on Danny, he refuses to abandon his responsiblity to the management. Wendy wants to stay in the hotel for her husband's sake, yet she knows that staying there means risking the welfare of herself and Danny. Aware of his father's obligations, Danny also wants to stay for Jack, yet he also recognizes that the longer they remain in the Overlook, the approaching doom draws nearer.

The three Torrances eventually draw into three separate corners as none can wholly fulfill the expectations of the others, expectations that threaten the individual well-being of each family member. This inability of the Torrances to act as an ideal family leads to their gradual separation from one another, which indeed supports King's notion that realistically the family is not the solution to all problems, and that to expect as much leads to disappointment and a reduction in dependency on the institution. It is only when Wendy and Danny reach the belated realization that the bond of their familial love can overcome Jack and the Overlook, that any family togetherness really occurs in the novel. Even then, the two barely escape disaster. As Burton Hatlen points out,

American mythology has not prepared us to see the family as a cauldron of hate; to recover such a view of the family, we must go back to Aeschylus or Shakespeare. Nevertheless, *The Shining* insists that we see the family as a deeply ambiguous phenomenon, at once a blessing and a curse. (93)

Because the Torrances cannot achieve a balance between pleasing both themselves and the family unit, tragedy unwinds. Jack, Wendy, and Danny are all caught in the crunch born of feeling the need to compromise their personal interests for the sake of the larger family institution.

Since King does not observe the family as flawless in meeting each of its members' needs, people in King's fiction must often bond with someone outside of the family for moral support. This outside bonding is regularly seen among King's adolescents, who often turn to their families for assistance only to find disappointment or failure, a situation King feels young people fear most:

> Q: What's the greatest horror that you think high school kids face today?
>
> KING: Not being able to interact, to get along and establish lines of communication. It's the fear I had, the fear of not being able to make friends, the fear of being afraid and not being able to tell anyone you're afraid.... There's a constant fear that I am alone. Mentally, you feel you're running a fever. That's when people need a close relationship, especially outside the family. Inside the family things are often very tense: people say little more than "Please pass the butter" or "Give me the rolls." And all the time kids are deathly afraid that they won't be able to get along. (BB 89-90)

Because King is in tune with the alienation young Americans feel toward their families, he "often departs from the normal fictional portrayal of parent/child interactions to make the point that affinity and understanding are neither an innate property of parenthood nor antithetical to family situations" (Notkin 135).

Prime examples of King's young people who look outside of the family for bonding can be found in *'Salem's Lot, The Body, The Talisman*, and *It*. In *'Salem's Lot*, young protagonist Mark Petrie forms a bond with the adult Ben Mears when he comes to the understanding that his parents are unable to console his fears of the doom approaching his town. *The Talisman*, like *'Salem's Lot*, involves the joining of a child and a non-familial adult. In the story, young Jack Sawyer must turn to Speedy Parker, a black janitor working at the amusement park near his summer residence. Because Jack's father had been killed by his uncle, and because Jack's mother is rendered helpless by sickness, Speedy becomes the support Jack needs to complete his journey west in search of the talisman that will cure his mother and save her twin in the otherworldly Territories.

While *The Body* and *It* do not depict a child-adult union, the need for non-familial bonding is equally apparent. Throughout *The Body*, King discloses the extremely troubled family lives of the four boys, who turn to one another for the bonding needed to complete their rite of passage, a bonding they are unable to find within their homes. Similarly, the young people in *It* form a youth gang, The Loser's Club, in response to a lack of emotional fulfillment on the homefront. With the exception of Mike Hanlon and, to an extent, Bill Denbrough, each member of the gang comes from a dysfunctional family. Two characters in particular, Bev Marsh and Eddie Kapsbrack, both suffer from the tendencies of their disturbed parents: Bev's father is given to fits of rage that often include assault, while Eddie's mother is a hypochondriac who overnurtures her son, always believing Eddie is sick. The Loser's Club find in one another the friendship and bonding often denied them at their homes. As all four stories suggest, people in King's fiction often need to turn their affections outside of the family in order to obtain the moral and mental support often expected and not realized by the family; societal institutions in the books seek more to control and discourage these young people than allow them to obtain self-fulfillment. The non-familial unions they formulate allow King's characters to interact with others in search of autonomy.

As all of the preceding examples have aimed to prove, King is ambiguous about an individual's relationship with larger societal institutions; United States governmental bodies are not free from his scrutiny. He appears in his writing to be equivocal regarding the role of constituents under a democratic government. While his characters are often beriddled with matters of their own subjectivity, they are also sometimes pursued by the demands of governmental interests seeking to establish order. One story in particular, *The Aftermath*, an unpublished story written when King was in high school, thoroughly explores the dilemma between individual freedom and conformity to government's rules and regulations. The story is about the condition of American society after an atomic war has reduced much of it to ashes. The war tears down most of America's pre-war structures and institutions. For a period of time, the country is in a state of anarchy with no leading body to direct it. Soon an organization called the Sun Corps, a military operation that intends to restore societal order, begins to grow. The story's protagonist, Larry Talman, tries desperately to stay clear from the organization as he finds comfort in the true individual freedom resulting from the government's collapse. The anarchy the Sun Corps aims to control allows Talman to temporarily understand the human condition as it exists in his present world as compared to the pre-atomic America—an orderly, controlled society that ultimately repressed individuality:

Talman knew nothing of the Sun Corps, but enough to know he wanted no part of them. He wanted no part of any organized body from here on out. When men started organizing, that's when the trouble began. One group led to another, and every group had its own cock-of-the-walk leader, it's [sic] own little Caeser [sic].... That's all government amounted to, Talman thought. A bunch of gangsters lording it over the square joes [sic]. That's all the United States and Russia ever were despite all their fine propoganda. (12-13)

As Talman continues to remain sovereign, avoiding the Sun Corps, he eventually befriends another fugitive, Ian Vannerman, who has confidential knowledge of the Corps that prompts him to suggest he and Talman unite in infiltrating and destroying it. The two set out to accomplish this by signing up with the Corps, which will bring them inside the organization, where they can begin to dismantle it. While on the inside, they learn that the Corps advertises itself as being for the benefit of the people but that its primary motive is to restore social order at any cost; rebels and anarchists are executed. The longer Talman interacts with other Corpsmen, the more he understands the irony of trying to crumble the operation:

Sheep, Talman thought. All a bunch of stupid sheep waiting to be shorn. He was suddenly very angry that by destroying the Corps he and Vannerman would be doing the sheep a favor, too. The boot lickers and the I'm-a-good boy-pat-my-head types. (49)

He realizes that by unravelling the Corps, he would set free the same people whose submission to societal order allows such organizations to exist.

Talman and Vannerman ultimately destroy the Corps, which turns out to be a front for a group of aliens that were capitalizing on humankind's ultimate screw-up, nuclear war. The aliens had seen and acted upon both Americans' tendency to self-destruct and their need to be governed because of that tendency. By shaping these shortcomings to their advantage, the aliens were using the Corps as a vehicle for extra-terrestrial domination on earth, a subplot King uses to comment on the lack of personal direction in America that leads to people's manipulation.

In the end, once their adversaries are defeated, Talman and Vannerman return to wandering the American wasteland. At one point in their journey, Vannerman, a member of the Espers, a breed of psychics evolving after the war, discloses to his comrade that the Espers are preparing their own attempt at organizing society. Talman's despair is heightened once again as he recognizes he'd partaken in preventing a suppressive societal order only to be introduced to an equally threatening scheme afterwards. He acknowledges that humankind simply cannot live as sovereign individuals but insists on being governed.

Vannerman departs to join the Espers in their planning, leaving Talman to roam alone just as he did at the beginning of the story. Once again in isolation, Talman realizes that he will ultimately need the benefits of social order and institutions, even if they make him a supplicant like the majority of the population, something he ponders as he begins to walk in search of civilization:

The people were probably on their knees begging to be governed. Please, the people said. I will let you take my freedom and my dignity and my individuality if you will feed me. I will sell my children into bondage if you find me a place to sleep. I will pay your taxes and give lip service to your government if you provide a toilet so I won't have to squat in the woods.... You say you know the evils of government, his mind whispered. But are the evils of government any worse than the evils of anarchy? I like anarchy just fine. Sure, you do. But what about the pregnant woman that must have her baby alone? What about the man with the gangrenous leg, and no one to help him live or die? What about you, when you get old and can't move so fast? Government is wrong! He shouted in his mind. The War showed that. The Sun Corps showed that. But he could see all the flaws in his argument now. His eyes were open, for better or for worse. (76)

He grasps the truth of people's need for a higher authority in an orderly society, despite the degree of conformity or suppression required. As King argues through the story, the needs met by societal institutions take precedence over individuality. Because the people in *The Aftermath* cannot achieve simultaneity between autonomy and a positive relationship with larger society, the overview of humanity is dreary.

While King highlights the evils of societal institutions in their tendency to suppress individuality, his accusations are most often aimed at them when they seek to implement order for selfish goals. In *The Aftermath*, the institutions King rebukes are not functioning for the welfare of their constituents but rather aim to control society as they please. Both the pre-war U.S. government and the Sun Corps act not on behalf of the people but for the augmentation of their own power. Because they do not heed the interests of the masses, they engage in egocentric power-plays, which are evident in the government's willingness to partake in nuclear war and the Sun Corps' execution of dissenters.

King provides an antithesis to *The Aftermath* in *The Stand*. In the novel, King presents a contrast not seen in the latter; he portrays the difference between an organization that is responsive to its constituents' needs and one that is self-serving, forfeiting the welfare of the people for power. After the flu epidemic that wipes out most of the American population, the survivors split into two groups: The Free Zone and those who follow the Dark Man, Randall Flagg. The Free Zone, led by the saintly Mother Abigail, is a society consisting of autonomous people wishing to bond together in good will; the only conformity required in the Free Zone is a universal participation in a meaningful community. The elected board of officials, The Free Zone Committee, responds to the people and does not use its influence for selfish gain. Flagg's army, on the other hand, exists only to destroy the Free Zone and the forces of good. What one sees in Flagg's community is not a union of autonomous people in a working society that recognizes their sovereignty but one bent on evil and destruction. This society, like the Sun Corps, responds to dissenters by executing them. People are discouraged from voicing their individual opinions, which when spoken often lead to death or incarceration. Conformity in Flagg's world requires the complete surrender of the self in support of the group's movement against the Zone. By juxtaposing these two opposites, King suggests that conformity to society does not demand a negative submission of the self as long as the society works together for the benefit of all, creating a togetherness that joins sovereign people with others who respect their individuality.

The preceding example provides an indication of the perks of participating in a society dedicated to the welfare of the whole, but King, in his usual fashion, does not let his reservations toward any form of social order go unexpressed. Even in the Free Zone, beneficent as it might be, people's innate distrust of others gradually begins to surface after the dissolution of Flagg's army. Once the Zoners are free of Flagg's threat and begin to spread throughout the country, they find the guns and weapons left behind by their enemies. They arm themselves, "just in case." Near the close of the story, Stu Redman explains that it was only a matter of time before the foundations of the Free Zone were distorted by people's general lack of faith in others:

What happens after you give guns to the deputies? he asked himself. What's the logical progression? And it seemed that it was the scholarly, slightly dry voice of Glen Bateman that spoke in answer. You give them bigger guns. And police cars. And when you discover a Free Zone community down in Chile or maybe up in Canada, you make Hugh Petrella the Minister of Defense just in case, and maybe you start sending out search parties, because after all— That stuff is lying around, just waiting to be picked up. (1148)

As in *The Aftermath*, *The Stand*'s conclusion expresses humans' inability to trust others. This culminates in a state ruled by military force, which tends to forsake individuality for the larger whole. In both stories, one suppressive institution is removed only to make way for another.

King has in the past gone so far as to argue in his fiction that when an accord cannot be reached between autonomy and societal conformity, it is better to be alone in facing the world than to be a pawn in a scheme of societal order. In *The Gunslinger*, the first installment of *The Dark Tower* series, the story opens with an isolatto, Roland, crossing a barren land in pursuit of "the man in black," who is the key to secrets of the universe Roland wishes to uncover. The novel creates an atmosphere of complete isolation as Roland receives the notion of bonding as burdensome in his quest. Even when he befriends Jake, a young boy he discovers at a way station, he comes to see him as an extra weight to carry despite his growing feelings of fondness for him. If one pays close attention to the novel's depictions of Roland travelling alone and Roland interacting with others in a community, one will find that the only times he is truly in jeopardy are when he is involved with others in an ordered group. King's first detailed description of Roland with a community comes when Roland enters the town of Tull while following the man in black. Tull is consisted of religious zealots who see Roland as an interloper, and, at the prompting of the man in black, who had crossed through Tull before Roland, they try to expel him, thinking him a demon spirit. They bear arms and move to kill him, an act of aggression to which he must respond by shooting them all until not one is left standing. The second instance in which Roland is seen in a community setting comes in the periodic descriptions of his interaction with his past world, a world where young men were trained to be gunslingers. This community likewise threatened Roland as it was a tightly constructed one based on harsh discipline in assuring that the trainees become highly efficient in their craft. At the close of the story, the reader can conclude that while Roland is indeed a lonely man, in light of the chaos arising from any contact with societal order, he is truly better off carrying out his quest without companions.

The conflict created between pursuing selfhood and conforming to larger societal institutions has been one recurrently explored by King's American literary predecessors. William Faulkner does it in *As I Lay Dying* while Flannery O'Connor touches the same issue in *Wise Blood* and *The Violent Bear It Away*. Faulkner's Bundren family embarks on a journey to bury mother/wife Addie, a task that calls for their togetherness, yet during the journey, their separation from one another grows more apparent. What the reader can see in the Bundren quest is not a group of individuals coming together to accomplish the quest but rather a group of individuals forced and cramped together, which intensifies their alienation from one another. The family's lack of unity and failure to create a bonding force results in the portrayals of Jewel's break from communication with his siblings, Darl's emotional breakdown, Vardaman's delusions about his dead mother, and Dewey Dell's lonely abortion. Instead of providing familial unity, the trek to bury Addie reinforces that the family journey only augments the Bundrens' personal troubles.

In the O'Connor novels, her characters are trapped in a society that perverts and distorts the human spirit, a condition to which her protagonists must react by severing all ties with humanity. *Wise Blood*'s Hazel Motes does this by blinding himself, which prohibits him from having to view the chaos of his world; *The Violent Bear It Away*'s Frank Tarwater achieves his breach from humanity by refusing to communicate with his uncle and cousin, whom he ultimately kills. At the end of both stories, the only way Motes and Tarwater can carry out their lives is by retreating into isolation separate from the rest of society, which can offer nothing but despair and discouragement.

Like the characters in the Faulkner and O'Connor novels, King's fictional people are often troubled by an inability to coordinate pursuit of autonomy with societal conformity. His characters are born of real Americans, who while in search of the virtues written by their founding fathers, are recurringly discouraged from achieving their personal goals by pressures to adhere to the expectations and demands of societal institutions. Through this portrayal of an American dilemma, King aims to show that while Americans must work together in maintaining a harmonious society, they must also allow themselves the opportunity to live out their lives with respect for their own interests. Without a balance between fulfillment of the self and involvement with larger groups in pursuit of a collective good will, the human condition in America will remain perpetually bleak.

VI. Survival in a Despairing World

A close reading of Stephen King's fiction indicates that there is widespread pain and suffering in the world mostly because of humankind's ignorance of the virtues essential in promoting a better human condition. In his books, greed, jealousy, envy, selfishness, and the hunger for power all take the places of the qualities that through their benign influence bind people together. After being presented the plethora of adversities causing people to fall from grace and humanity, one might wonder, when reading a King text, if anyone can survive at all in the absurd circus called Earth. What it all boils down to is that King, while blatantly displaying his pessimism and reservations toward human nature, does have faith in humanity. Aside from those recommendations for a better human condition mentioned thus far—a sound sense of morality, cherishing childhood memories, controlling the thirst for technological advance, abstaining from a selfish interpretation of capitalist ideology, and establishing a balance between autonomy and societal conformity—the main solution to all the pain and suffering in his fictional world is simple and easy to accept: stay close to loved ones, form strong bonds with dear friends, surrender the self to aid another; if people could consistently adhere to these basic requests, all the other recommendations could follow of their own accord. After all, the human misgivings as discussed to this point all result from a forfeit of fellowship. The fundamental need to bond with other people is as old as the Bible, and it remains significant in King's twentieth-century fiction because of its universal application to the human condition.

King is an adamant believer in the powers of love and self-sacrifice. He rarely strays from rewarding those who exercise these virtues with either personal or moral salvation or simple survival. Those characters who refuse to bond with others while in the pursuit of selfish goals are those who are punished or swallowed by evil. Both of these concepts occur repeatedly throughout King's canon. In *The Shining*, it is Jack Torrance's refusal to turn to his loved ones (his wife and son) when the Overlook threatens his spirit that culminates in his death. The scene in the Colorado Ballroom where Jack participates in a supernatural ball with past occupants of the hotel is but one key step in Jack's path to destruction: it is when he crosses the line between grasping or rejecting his love for Wendy. During a dance, he is approached by a mysterious woman, who appeals to his lust. Jack succumbs to his passion and allows himself to be taken in by the woman's appeal. Concerning this scene, Tony Magistrale points out that "King seems to be indicating here that in the dissipation of his marital commitment to Wendy, Torrance forsakes his only chance for survival" (MV 55).

The survivors in the novel are those who are willing to sacrifice themselves for others despite the risks of injury or death. Wendy, Danny, and Dick Hallorrann are able to persevere simply because they ultimately recognize that bonding together is the only way to defeat the Overlook as it tries to claim them, too; the bond enables them to escape from both the transfigured Jack and the Overlook, which burns to the ground in the finale. The story is also significant in that it creates a David and Goliath scenario: the white American male with the support of the Overlook's male history against the 'weaker' minorities of society and literature—a child, a woman, and a black. What King suggests in this novel is that when people come together for fellowship, it does not matter what places they hold in society; love and bonding wear no particular size, sex, or skin. The union of Wendy, Danny, and Hallorrann renders their minority statuses insignificant, making them larger than any evil opposing them.

Small-group bondings such as the one in *The Shining* appear often in King's fiction, reinforcing his notion that Good in any form, shape, or size is infinitely more powerful than evil. Victims of adversity do not need a supernatural proponent equal to that of their supernatural opponents. On the contrary, they can overcome their struggles through the coming together of a few people under tremendous stress willing to promote good, creating a transcendent aura of human love, something Burton Hatlen believes to be King's suggested key to survival:

In general, I would argue, the Good in King's world is represented only by such small groups of people who (barely) cling together in the face of encroaching darkness, rather than by any supernatural power which can serve to counter-balance the forces of destruction. (85)

As Hatlen so aptly points out, King often does not pull out psychic and supernatural powers to combat evil but rather aims to show that when it comes to opposing adversity, love and fellowship are formidable.

Although King believes in the unity of human beings under stress to oppose worldly and unworldly evil, one must recognize that King is aware that not all people have the means to establish such a bond. Some of King's characters set themselves apart from society because they have been conditioned to believe that everyone in society would rather see them perish. Two of King's earlier novels, *Carrie* and *Christine*, focus on such characters. Carrie White does not bond with others in the shadow of oncoming danger but rather becomes the oncoming danger as a result of being excluded from her social environment. Absolutely no one will help Carrie in her search for autonomy, a search which if fulfilled could aid in taming her psychic powers. Because she has no one to confide in, her powers run away with her, and she destroys a town. Carrie's story is the mirror opposite of King's romantic vision of human bonding—a story that attempts to illustrate that while people may join together and overcome evil through their combined love and friendship, people may become evil by being refused access to such interactions. As Douglas Winter argues, "the reader of Carrie should understand that evil lies not in Carrie White but in her tormentors— and, more important, in the traps of society and religious mania in which her tormentors are confined" (AOD 35). Carrie is the product of a society that has eroded the virtues of personal love and friendship in favor of mass organization and construction; she "is the first of many King protagonists who reflect his naturalistic stance— she starts nothing of her own free will. The fault—the evil—is that of nature itself, and of the artificial constructs of nature (her society and religion) that civilization has erected" (35).

Like Carrie, Arnie Cunningham starts nothing of his "own free will"; he is also similar to her in his alienation from peers and significant others. However, unlike Carrie, he has a means of resolution in Dennis Guilder, who, while much more popular than Arnie, tries to maintain his friendship with him. Arnie has become so conditioned to rejection that when he comes in contact with the '57 Plymouth Fury, the new sense of identity the car gives him takes priority even over his human bond with Dennis. Dennis attempts desperately to pull Arnie out of his rendez-vous with disaster, but Arnie, who seeks revenge on the society that has excluded him, becomes the perfect vehicle for the worldly hatred his automobile represents. His breach of faith in humanity leads him to isolate himself from the one person who truly cares about him, and who could, through the bonds of friendship, save him from imminent doom. It is Arnie's rejection of Dennis' extended hand of fellowship that culminates in both his death and the deaths of several others.

Some of the strongest bonds in King's fiction come out of unions made outside of the family, much like the one offered Arnie by Dennis Guilder. While it has previously been argued that such relationships may stem from the inability of family members to live up to the nurturance expected of them, one may also reasonably argue that such relationships provide reassurance that humans may bond with others not related directly to them. King often seems to find the idea of people not connected by blood ties coming together more significant because there is usually an element of sacrifice involved—a sacrifice that one makes not because one is expected to, as in the nuclear family, but because one wants to. The non-familial relationships in King's fiction arise from the need to connect with humans regardless of their modes of connection.

The union of children with adults outside of the family appears to be especially powerful to King not only because it is a joining of humanity but also because it creates a working synthesis between the intellectual capacities of the two age groups; the unbridled imagination of the young and the wisdom of the older produces a balance that both may learn from, creating a wholeness that allows for a more complete union capable of battling adversities. Rather than combining young with young (*It* and *The Body*) and old with old, resulting in a homogenous but not whole joining of minds, King employs the young with the old because opposing danger often requires a combination of imagination and experience. In *It* and *The Body*, the protagonists are all youths and overcome adversity through the strength of their bonding, but their battle is intensified because they do not have the worldly know-how characteristic of adults.

Two fine examples of King's union between a child and a non-familial adult, examples which have already been discussed to an extent, are found in *'Salem's Lot* and *The Shining*, where the bonding becomes the combination necessary for turning back the approaching danger. In both cases, an imaginative child is joined with an experienced adult, and each is able to absorb from the other what he did not have before they came together. Deborah Notkin describes King's utility of these types of unions as giving his writing an inspirational flavor:

When an author portrays children as human beings in their own right, it is not at all surprising when they form bonds with people who are not their parents, nor even their parents' friends. These bonds, throughout King's work, are formed out of human responses rather than artificial age divisions, and help to make both the child characters and the books themselves more plausible and more interesting. *The Shining*, once again, ends with the bonds formed by such human responses, after affirming (through the self-sacrifice of Dick Hallorrann) King's belief that people will risk their lives for one another. (136)

The romanticism of King's unions between children and adults is an uplifting departure from the American media's recurrent portrayal of a conflict between young and old, a conflict bred of the age division that prohibits them from a working communication. These bonds highlight King's belief that human beings need not be separated because of discernible characteristics; on the contrary, the child-adult combinations suggest that people of any sort can come together as one powerful representation of the goodness within the human spirit. As Notkin observes of these fusions, "such non-familial, non-sexual love relationships are rare in literature and rarer still in genre fiction" (134).

While King illustrates the magnificence of non-familial bonding in pursuit of good will, he also presents the antithesis of such bonds when they are formulated not out of a benign concern for others but for selfish or manipulative motives. Such a union can be seen in the novella *Apt Pupil* (*Different Seasons*). The story also depicts a relationship between a child and a non-familial adult, but this relationship is a parasitic one, one in which the two suck the vitality from each other rather than augment it. It begins because of young Tod Bowden's desire to uncover the dark secrets of Nazi concentration camps, secrets held by a neighbor, Kurt Dussander, who was once a Nazi officer. When Dussander initially refuses to satiate Tod's thirst for this information, Tod blackmails him by threatening to disclose to authorities that this war criminal, one searched by U.S. and Jewish officials for years, lives right down the street from him. Dussander has no choice but to comply. However, Dussander eventually catches Tod in his own trap as he realizes Tod has been lying to his parents about the nature of his frequent visits with the older man, who Tod's parents are led to believe is in need of nurturance in his old age. Were Dussander to reveal to Mr. and Mrs. Bowden Tod's fabrication of the truth, Tod would discover himself in trouble. Because both Dussander and Tod have information that could injure the other, they are forced to stay together as neither trusts the other to keep his secrets. As the relationship progresses, they are both catapulted into a world of dread. Tod's uncovering of Dussander's tainted past reawakens it, creating the need for Dussander to kill once again as he did under Hitler. Likewise, because of his constant exposure to Dussander's regressions and because of his excess knowledge of one of the darkest chapters in human history, Tod is pulled into Dussander's nightmare and also turns to killing. Through this portrayal of a cannibalistic relationship where both parties eat the other's spirit, King shows the dark side of bonding when the bond is made of bad intent rather than of a need for human fellowship in support of good will.

As the preceding examples show, King has succeeded in portraying the power of non-familial relationships when made with benevolence. He does not completely ignore the impact of familial bonding but rather treats it as some of the most magical moments in his fiction. When family members in King's stories are able to break through their scrambled channels of communication, the results are often significant in their later implications. Two such occurrences appear in *Christine* and *The Sun Dog*. In *Christine*, the relationship between Dennis Guilder and his father serves as the mirror opposite of the one between Arnie and his father. Where Arnie and his father are engaged in perpetual conflict and misunderstanding that reinforce their alienation from each other, Dennis and his father have a meaningful father-son relationship that Dennis cherishes and often turns to in times of crisis. While Arnie does not have trust enough in his father to discuss his problems with him, thinking he will dip into the well of reason to find all the solutions, Dennis' bond with his father exists on a gut-level; the accord between them allows Dennis to bring his troubles to his father, who provides thoughtful answers. In fact, King's portrayal of the relationship between the Guilders strongly reflects what King, who grew up without a father, imagines the wonder of such relationships to be—feelings he explicates through Dennis when Dennis recalls a heart-to-heart talk he'd had with his father:

There was a moment of electric communication between us—even now, four years later, I get goose bumps thinking about it, although I'm by no means sure that I can get it across to you. It wasn't that he treated me like an equal for the first time that night; it wasn't even that he was showing me the wistful knight-errant still hiding inside the button-down man scrambling for a living in a dirty, hustling world. I think it was sensing him as a reality, a person who had existed long before I ever came onstage, a person who had eaten his share of mud. In that moment I think I could have imagined him making love to my mother, both of them sweaty and working hard to make it, and not have been embarrassed. (120)

This passage implies the impact a strong familial bond can create; it is the openness of the relationship between Dennis and his father that propels Dennis to muster his courage later when confronting Christine.

In *The Sun Dog*, King again reveals his romantic notion of a powerful father-son bond, much like the one exemplified by the Guilders. Young Kevin Delevan's relationship with his father serves to counter his relationship with the rest of the adult world, which the avaricious Pop Merrill embodies. While there still remains a gap between Kevin and his father in his father's inability to perceive the looming danger from an imaginative child's perspective, it is his father's willingness to bond with his son that provides the chemistry for defeating the evil dog behind the lens of Kevin's Polaroid Sun 660. Mr. Delevan is able to see Kevin as a living, impressionable branch of himself, a realization that allows him to at least attempt to address his son's predicament. A scene such as the following illustrates Mr. Delevan's compassion for his son, compassion shown in a situation where Kevin approaches his father with his concerns about the camera, and his father, preoccupied with other matters, responds:

He was preoccupied with this, already talking to Brandon Reed in his mind, but not so preoccupied he didn't see the gratitude which lighted his son's worried face. Mr. Delevan smiled a little and felt that uncharacteristic gloom first ease and then let go entirely. There was this much, at least: his son was as yet not too old to take comfort from him, or accept him as a higher power to whom appeals could sometimes be directed in the knowledge that they would be acted upon; nor was he himself too old to take comfort from his son's comfort. (727)

Feelings such as Mr. Delevan's support King's belief that the family does not need to be a "cauldron of hate" but rather can include relationships of significant meaning. By reaching out to his son and offering his guidance, Mr. Delevan becomes an element in a union that proves uncontestable in battling the dreadful Sun Dog.

King illustrates the tragedy that can result from forsaking familial bonding to present a whole picture. "The Last Rung on the Ladder"

(*Night Shift*) shows the dreadful fate of a man's sister when the man drifts from her in pursuit of his own interests. When a boy Larry had lived on a farm with his family. One day his parents had left both him and his sister, Katrina, alone while running errands. A favorite game of Larry's and Katrina's had been to climb a ladder to the top of their barn and dive off into stacks of hay. On the day they were alone, the ladder had snapped when Katrina was near the top, nearly seventy feet from the ground. Larry had run about desperately trying to collect enough hay to build a pile that would soften Katrina's fall. Katrina had held on for dear life until she could hold no longer. When she did fall, there had been enough hay beneath her to save her life; the only injury sustained was a broken ankle.

As the years pass by, and the siblings evolve into adults, Larry becomes totally enveloped in his own life and career as a successful lawyer. His sister, on the other hand, is suffering from severe emotional problems and has no one to confide in. She tries repeatedly to contact Larry by writing him letters. Larry, always busy, fails to respond. Katrina ultimately dives from her high-rise apartment to her death far below; she had thought the hay would be there.

Whether it involves a same-aged peer, a non-familial adult, a sibling, or a parent, King regularly portrays a vision of humanity where simple love and fellowship between human beings reigns victorious over adversity. The fact that King's resolution is pervasive in his fiction offers an optimistic perspective of humanity non-existent in the significant fiction of many of his American literary predecessors. The portraits of humanity seen in fictions by Flannery O'Connor, William Faulkner, and Joyce Carol Oates could not wish to have the faith in humanity contained in King's stories. Whether it be O'Connor's Hazel Motes or Frank Tarwater, Faulkner's Bundren family, or Oates' "In the Region of Ice" or "Where Are You Going? Where Have You Been?", all three writers present a human condition where bonding with human beings is almost impossible in a distraught, bleak world. In these stories, isolation and despair are the rule rather than the exception.

By displaying a faith in the potential of human beings to create positive bonds with others, King provides a satisfying resolution to all the shortcomings of human nature. Through renouncing their tendencies to isolate themselves in pursuit of personal gain, King's Americans can transcend the suffering inherent in the human condition and once and for all grasp the true magic of being alive in a world where there are others willing to reciprocate love and friendship for the sake of righteousness and good will.

Epilogue: The End of the Journey

The hardest part of this journey through Stephen King's America is knowing where to end it. The people and places that we've seen together on this trip have shown us something about ourselves and the country we live in. They've shown us that literary content is often separated only by its varying surfaces; the concerns beneath are universally the same. The human experience and the written expression of it never really end; they only metamorphosize as they continue to evolve.

Having been educated in English literature, I am cognizant of the major works by the twentieth century's major artists. I see those same qualities that established his literary predecessors' greatness in Stephen King's fiction. The themes found within his books are those that were expressed years before he began writing—they are as relevant to the need to understand the human condition as anything produced before him. The only truly discerning characteristic between King's modern fiction and that written in the past is that he has changed the manifest to reflect the concerns and issues of today's society.

While one characteristic connecting King to his literary heritage is a naturalistic stance of a world being eroded both physically and emotionally by a human race without compassion, he, like he does when discussing any area of the human condition, goes one step further in suggesting that there is a way to create a breach in the isolation characteristic of modern literature. This extra dimension that King adds to the wasteland so often portrayed by modernists is representative of the notion of literature once expressed by poet William Carlos Williams, who saw the English language not as being required to adhere to traditional subject and form but needing to be constantly reworked as dictated by the thoughts and feelings of the present time. Then, and only then, would the English language break down the barriers of communication created by adherence to past literary trends and establish a dialect capable of relevant interpretation. King has done exactly so by using modern American colloquial language and augmenting the themes of his modernist

110

predecessors by including subject material and themes popular with his contemporary audience. As required of a significant artist, King has not abandoned the influence of the writers who most affected him but has reshaped the thoughts and feelings of past generations to accommodate the present; this in itself should be noteworthy of King's overwhelming contribution to present-day literature, a contribution that has not been fully recognized because of his placement in the popular-culture entertainment arena.

My motivation for writing this study of Stephen King's fiction arose directly from the realization that even though he has established himself as a leading artist, King has recurrently been regarded as a "popular-culture hack." The first time I picked up a Stephen King book, I did it not because I wanted to be led through a journey of the human experience but rather because I, like most people who read his books, wanted to be scared. However, as I hope this text proves, there is indeed a substance beneath the terror-ridden surface that dives much deeper than simple fear; it plunges into that inner core of the American heart that recognizes the inherent suffering and pain of being alive. The fact that King chose horror as a vehicle to comment on the human condition most likely has played the largest role in the dismissal of his work as serious art. But regardless of the criticism about his work, King seems to have found great comfort writing horror fiction at the speed of an F-14. No matter how he is received by his critics, he seems to be content with tales of terror, seeing no other way to express his feelings about humanity, which in reality is plagued by horrors much worse than those on the written page. As Deborah Notkin suggests, "Terror becomes a force which forges bonds though its purpose is to break them, which teaches love even while it loosens bowels. King holds out the hope that, if fear doesn't kill you, it leaves you with something invaluable which you could not otherwise attain" (134).

At the very least, if one cannot recognize the importance of King's contribution to and extension of American literature, one can observe King as a contemporary commentator of significance. By plucking real-life issues and concerns and holding them in front of his readers' eyes, he shapes the thoughts, feelings, and language of contemporary America into a trenchant work of fiction that becomes a journal of his American readers' lives. The prevalent themes in King's fiction—the dilemmas of moral choice, the need to remember younger years, the fear of untamed technological advance, the pursuit of wealth that dehumanizes people, the fear of subordinating personal interests to larger societal bodies—are all issues that have had a significant impact on every American's life. While King is able to present our world to us in way which we can understand, he gives us inspiration by suggesting that while we almost always fall by becoming too enveloped in the trivialities of modern society, we can avoid this by simply coming together to share in love, good will, and fellowship. After all,

we live in a time when the most natural response to all but our most immediate associates seems to be hate and distrust. There is little confidence in our future or even as a race. King, who belittles none of our fears, sounds a note of hope to counter them. If we can trust each other, hope is never lost. Stephen King is one of the few writers today, in any field, whose primary theme is one of hope and survival, despite the odds. In this light, his popularity is predictable, and perhaps his large audience is in itself a small portent of hope for the future. (Notkin 142)

As both a fan and an appreciator of the written word, I hope that Stephen King remains on the track he has taken to his stardom. A positive reception by critics, academics, and intellectuals is of little importance to this presentation, but it is the critical pounding King has often taken from these people that has led to discouraging others from reading his work more closely. I can only wish that people would stop trying to measure King against Shakespeare, Dickens, or any other literary giant. While I have argued that the connections are there, I believe that an overpursuit of such apparent connections shifts the emphasis from reading King's works for what they are to rebuking them for what they aren't. After all, anything current seems weak when held up to the past; popular culture fiction—in this case, King's fiction—needs to sit like wine, just as Shakespeare's or Dickens' works needed to sit, so that it may ferment, becoming more sweet to the taste for future generations. Critics and academics have always longed for the past; they have always looked backwards in search of a gem representing 'true' art, a gem that receives its greatness because the generational gap has given it the proper amount of time to be appreciated. King, like Dickens and Shakespeare did, speaks the language of the people, and the colloquial language of one generation becomes the respected language of the next; critics have never failed to slam a present dialect. Like the wine that sits for years waiting to be tasted, the maturity of King's fiction will require years of fermentation in the literary archives. If history continues to repeat itself, forty or fifty years from now King may well be used as the barometer of greatness. Time will only tell.

I hope that reading this text will show you that there is much to be learned and experienced from Stephen King aside from enjoying his value as an entertainer. By showing the relationship between King and other significant twentieth-century American authors, I wanted to bring the content of Stephen King's fiction to a new group of readers. In a time and age where sitcoms, heavy-metal rock stars, costumed slashers, and foul-mouthed comedians are leading figureheads of popular culture, King's fiction enables the contemporary American to participate in an experience concerning humanity, an experience that may last long after it has been completed.

My research and reading have pulled me into his world, and like a long-lost father, he took me by the hand and led me on a journey through the experience, one that I expect him to continue long after this text has been completed. In a way, my excursion into Stephen King's horrific realm was a belated rite of passage, one which taught me what it is to be a living, active member of America, and one which allowed me to escape from the daily rituals of living to look back on them and observe them with scrutiny. I hope that you too will be able to recognize the powerful American commentary within his fiction and allow Stephen King the opportunity to share with you his visions of the human condition. I hope that your next reading of him smacks home with all the vitality and wonder of being alive.

We've come to the end of this particular road. But let me assure you, it's one that continues far beyond where this one stops. King's tour of America never ends but rather continues to traverse its terrain in search of new discoveries of self. The places and people discovered while on Stephen King's fictional transport may be received in different ways, but one thing is for sure: they belong to us.

Part Three:

The Interviews

Author's Note

When I began the research for this book, I knew that speaking with people knowledgeable about the fine points of Stephen King's work would be an excellent supplementation. I located four individuals: Tony Magistrale (University of Vermont), Carroll Terrell (University of Maine at Orono), Burton Hatlen (also from UMO), and Gary Hoppenstand (Michigan State University). All four have either had personal contact with King or have performed extensive scholarship on his fiction. The information I collected from these men surpassed my highest expectations as each was able to shine a pleasantly distinct light on Stephen King's work.

The issue soon became whether to incorporate relevant material from the interviews into my thesis or to include the interviews in their entirety; both approaches appeared sufficient. However, as my research brought to my attention almost all of the books written about Stephen King, I've become aware that I have yet to find a book where several voices are prominently heard without the formalities of an argumentative essay. To present the interviews in their fullness will make my book what I hope to be the first of many where men who have dedicated their time, passion, and efforts into reading and understanding the power of Stephen King's storytelling are able to express their truest feelings about him in a conversational tone.

My research began from a purely academic standpoint with the intent of proving Stephen King's literary greatness; it wasn't until several weeks into my studies that I decided to center my thesis on his American themes. Because I initially embarked on a journey to match Stephen King with other great writers of the twentieth century, there are a great deal of questions in the interviews that probe the relationship between King and his prominent American literary predecessors. However, early on, I was lucky enough to have at least had an inkling of the American flavor of his fiction to elicit responses to his recurrent American themes, themes which I gained a greater grasp of as my research and questions evolved. Regardless, the interviews provide satisfying accounts of King as both a literary force and an American commentator.

Some of the information within the interviews supports what I have already argued; some of it tends to either debate or call to question major points of my thesis. Whatever the side that is taken, the written voices of the four following men provide a refreshing reading experience for all Stephen King fans. But most importantly, the inclusion of those voices gives an indication of the growing interest in Stephen King as a major artist of our time.

I. **Tony Magistrale**, University of Vermont. Tony earned his B.A. degree from Allegheny College in Meadville, Pennsylvania, where he majored in English. As a Mellon Fellow at the University of Pittsburgh, he earned both an M.A. and Ph.D. After completing his training, he won a Fulbright post-doctoral fellowship to the Universita di Milano, Italy. Tony is currently an Associate Professor of English at UV where he directs the freshman composition program and teaches courses in American literature. He is one of the very few college instructors in the U.S. who teaches an entire course for credit on Stephen King's fiction. He is also the author of two books on Stephen King—*Landscape of Fear: Stephen King's American Gothic* (Bowling Green State University Popular Press, 1988) and *The Moral Voyages of Stephen King* (Starmont House, 1989)—and has edited another book analyzing King's fiction, *"The Shining"* Reader (Starmont House, 1990). Tony has recently completed writing a book for the Twayne United States Authors Series, *Stephen King, The Second Decade*: Danse Macabre *to* The Dark Half.

This interview was conducted orally in July, 1991.

JD: It seems that an academic elite in this country has produced an exclusive canon of authors in the field of literature. As an English professor, tell me what qualities go into classic writing. In other words, what makes a great writer?

TM: There are two definitions that make up what I would call a definition of a classic writer. First of all it would be the quality of the work as measured by the people who take it seriously, read it carefully, write about it, talk about it, and think about it. The second is germane to an academic definition of a classic work in its ability to endure. If a work endures over a period of time, it becomes a classic. People feel the need to have to teach it and read it and reread it and analyze it.

JD: When you say endure, do you mean that a person who picked it up forty years ago would be as affected by the work if he/she were to pick it up today?

TM: No, I think that books change, the meanings change, over time. A book has different meanings to us as time develops, depending upon how we view things. How we come to give a context to the book itself is relevant to its meaning that it will have at a specific period of time. You're seeing that to be very much the case in the last twenty years as people are re-evaluating or re-interpreting works by Shakespeare, for instance, from a context that is decidedly different than the one that he was originally read in and listened to during the Renaissance. This is the age of feminism and New Historicism, and it is in the context of understanding Shakespeare as a social and political writer, understanding Shakespeare as a writer who discusses gender tensions and differences, that he is now being read. This was not the case during the Renaissance; these were issues that they were not concerned with. During the Renaissance they were more concerned with Shakespeare's cosmological perspective on things—where things fit in in terms of the relationship between man and nature and God, and of course the king.

JD: Aside from Stephen King's commercial success, what is it about his works of fiction that causes the academic elite to shut the door on him?
TM: That's a good question because the problem for many of the academic elite—and I say that with a certain degree of scorn because those people who view themselves as elitists in whatever field they're in are not the kind of people who I have much discourse with because I find them very pretentious and not worthy of much conversation—who dismiss King do so primarily because they've never read him. In failing to read him or about him because they think anybody who's popular can't be any good, they don't understand that there's more than just blood and guts—there's more than just the Gothic roller coaster ride—at work in his fiction. They're not open to the subtexts because they haven't even read the texts. They're oblivious to the various social, political, technological, historical subtexts that continually find their way into his fiction.

JD: What drew you to King's work in the first place? When and where did you get started?
TM: I think it was always my fascination with the Gothic. When I was an undergraduate at Allegheny College, I had a professor there whose name was F. S. Frank. Frank was and is a very brilliant man, and his orientation was primarily centered on the Gothic. He believed that because the Gothic has always been a popular literature, if you're truly going to understand the history of a particular time that you need to go to its most popular literature. The Gothic has always been popular and thus reflects certain tendencies

about the given culture that it has emerged from. He taught me how to think in terms of a social context for understanding works of popular fiction. Of course when you look at *Frankenstein*, Poe, and Nathaniel Hawthorne from this context, the reasons for their popularity in the nineteenth century were different than why they are popular now.

As I got older, I went to graduate school, still kept my fascination with the Gothic because Frank had taught me in so many classes, and ended up writing a dissertation on Flannery O'Connor, where I spent a good deal of time talking about the spiritual grotesque and patterns of spiritual revelation that are revealed through the Gothic trappings that run throughout her fiction. For me it's always been a logical connection from the world of *Frankenstein* and *Dracula* to Flannery O' Connor and William Faulkner to Stephen King and Peter Straub.

JD: So was there a particular first exposure that drew the connection between King and the aforementioned authors?
TM: I think the first thing that attracted me about King was that he's a damn good storyteller, and this is one of the things that the academic elite is missing out on—the fact that he gives you a very, very good ride in his best fiction.

JD: Well, it's like what other scholars interested in King often say about him: that he may not always feel comfortable with everything he writes but he never cheats his readers, never leaves the reader short of anything.
TM: Well sometimes he does. His less effective work does that. I think a novel that I felt very cheated after reading was *The Dark Half*—I just didn't think it worked at all.

JD: *The Tommyknockers?*
TM: I felt cheated in the last quarter of *The Tommyknockers*. I felt a little cheated in the last hundred pages of *The Talisman*. But then Stephen King's endings are never very good. You don't read Stephen King for the endings; you read Stephen King for the journey—the journey that has within it lots of truths about modern American life and about the human heart.

JD: Being an instructor of Stephen King's literature, how valuable do you think the incorporation of his literature would be to English curriculums? How likely is this of happening?

TM: It's extremely valuable, and it's extremely important for a number of reasons. The first one that comes to mind for me is that you can immediately capitalize on King's popularity. We live in a post-literate society; nobody reads any more. When we do read, and when we do find students interested in something, we ought to encourage that. One of the ways in which you can encourage students to read and become better readers and better literary critics is to give them stuff that they like. I think this is especially true at the high school level. I think it's very critical because if you get people excited about literature at that point or at any point, they're likely to go on and read other things; they won't just stop with Stephen King. So these quasi educators who feel that the students need to be purged from things that they enjoy reading and made to read things that are 'good' for them like *Julius Caesar, Silas Marner* or *Ethan Fromme*, these are individuals who are really killing the desire for knowledge rather than stimulating it.

JD: And perhaps weeding out potential English students?
TM: The hell with that. I'm interested in getting students thinking and excited about anything whether they decide to major in English or not. I just want them stimulated, thinking.

The motivation to be students on any level is dying rapidly. I mean, look at the attrition rate that we have in high schools nowadays. It's very bad, and one of the reasons for that is because we're still asking students to do things that we've been asking students to do for the last forty years. We haven't woken up to the fact that maybe we need to connect with them on things that are important to them. Certainly the numbers Stephen King puts up indicate that he's pretty important to them.

JD: Tell me what you see as being the prime motivations that propel an author to write a body of fiction.
TM: I don't know if I can do that. I think it depends on the writer. It depends upon what he/she has experienced. It depends on their view of the world. A body of fiction usually has some points that connect the different individual works into some sort of totality, and those connecting points are very much related to how a writer views the world, so they are as personal and individual as the human beings who are producing them.

JD: Why do you suppose that King's motivations for a work, which are significant in his interpretations of American society, are often overlooked by the general reading public? In other words, a person like me who has been trained to probe beneath the manifest can find King's themes readily apparent while the average poolside reader might skip right over them.

TM: I think it's because even in his best fiction he is subtle. I think it's also because a lot of people have not been trained to read carefully; not everybody is walking around here with a degree in English, which is fine. But if you're going to pick up on some—certainly not all—of the subtleties in a writer's work, you need to have training. You have to be taught how to think about something and how to read something carefully.

JD: Would you say the influence the media has had over the public during the last twenty or thirty years has had an influence over the way people read? The media has taught us to move quickly—things are at a fast pace.

TM: I think that's probably true; I think there's probably a lot to that. We do come from a society that is a throw-away culture, a society that is into fast food and emphasizes speed and economy. I suppose that's what we look for in our reading, too, and that's one of the reasons why King is so popular. He's an extremely accessible writer. So many young people like him because he doesn't really pose serious problems within the narrative, although some of his narratives are very complex—something like *It*, for instance, and the way in which the narrative fluctuates in that novel, moving in time sequences from past to present and vice versa.

JD: Would you classify King's contribution to literature on the same scale as say Faulkner or Shakespeare?

TM: I was at a conference about six years ago, and Leslie Fiedler, who is probably one of the most eminent American scholars writing today and without a doubt somebody who's attempted to revolutionize the way in which we read in the last twenty years, argued that fifty years from now the writer that we will be reading by way of telling the history of current contemporary America will be Stephen King. Fiedler firmly believes that King will not only endure but he will become the barometer for measuring the eighties and nineties. I subscribe to that, too. There are certain books in King's canon like *The Shining*, *Misery*, and possibly *The Stand* that will endure whether they were written by Stephen King or anyone else. It doesn't matter who wrote them; these are fine, fine books that are going to hold up over time.

JD: What immediate parallels can be drawn between what King writes and what someone like Faulkner or O'Connor once wrote?

TM: I guess the logical connection with Faulkner and O'Connor is in terms of regionalism. Stephen King is as much a regional writer about middle-class life in rural Maine as Faulkner was about the South and O'Connor was about the rural South. All of these writers' uses of regionalism provides distinctly unique perspectives on particular sections of the country. They also have qualities of permanence to them because they also open out to talk about characteristics that we all share in common; only they do it with a very, very regional flavor: a sense of place, setting, landscape, sense of time and the history of its relationship to the present. Faulkner was obsessed with the Civil War. O'Connor's "Good Country People" are obsessed with ways of doing things that are holdovers from the antebellum past and the challenge to that comes from her intellectuals.

JD: What similarities or differences do you see in the ways that Faulkner and O'Connor treated the white/black issue and the way King treats it?

TM: I think it's more complicated in Faulkner and O'Connor, particularly in Faulkner. I think Faulkner was more ambivalent in his relationship to blacks. It's not until Faulkner's late works—*Intruder in the Dust*—that we really see a black character who is independent-minded and capable of asserting his identity and humanity. There are no blacks like that in Flannery O'Connor. O'Connor's blacks are really there as vehicles to the plot; they're there for the evolution of the white character. Her blacks are not very independent beings.

King's blacks are the opposite in that they're very admirable characters. All of his blacks—Mother Abigail, Dick Hallorann, Mike Hanlon—they're all very strong characters and very positively portrayed. But King's own perspectives on his black characters say to us that there's still some work to be done, that he hasn't created the kind of complexity in black fictional characters that he wishes to do.

JD: I think the same can be said for his women characters.

TM: Yeah, but what do you want from someone who's living in Bangor, Maine? It's pretty tough to create authentic black characters when you probably don't know any blacks.

JD: One cannot deny that King has achieved commercial success in gigantic proportions. What separates him from other current popular writers such as Danielle Steele, Jackie Collins, and V.C. Andrews, who all fall into the category of 'poolside' authors? What substance do you see that is non-existent in the latter?

TM: Yeah, I think that's true—that there's substance in King's work that's lacking in the others. I think if you read somebody like Jackie Collins or V. C. Andrews, the only thing you get is a superficial plot line. I don't think there's a lot of depth there.

JD: No social commentary?

TM: I don't think there's much of a social commentary, and if there is one in say somebody like Jackie Collins, it's that the rich are pigs, and they act like pigs, but that at the same time they're kind of exciting to watch. Reading Jackie Collins to me is like reading *People* magazine—you read it for a cheap fix, a cheap high, and when you put it down, you forget it. It doesn't stay with you, it doesn't endure. Maybe that's another way of defining what a classic piece of fiction is—something that stays with you. Like a good meal, it makes you want to digest it, think about it, and remember it with fondness.

JD: And years later, you'll turn back to it.

TM: And years later perhaps you'll want to duplicate the experience. When you read somebody like Jackie Collins, it's like ordering a pizza or a hamburger—you do it because at the time it's gratifying, and once it's over, there's not much that you want to savor. What comes back is more a greasy memory.

JD: Do you suppose King's easily accessible style is what causes him to be classified among pop-fiction rather than classic literature? Do you suppose that academics realize King can be picked up and enjoyed by a junior-high student, giving ground for skepticism toward King as a serious artist?

TM: That probably has something to do with it. But I think when you're talking about English teachers, professors, who are finally the custodians of culture, you're talking about people who are pretty hard to please. In many cases you're talking about people who really indulge in fantasies of elitism. That's really unfortunate because some of the best writers who ever lived, people like Poe, Twain, Dickens or Shakespeare, are individuals who can also be picked up by junior high school students and read and appreciated and enjoyed. One can pick up *Great Expectations* and enjoy it.

It seems to me that when we're talking about King's popularity and his standing with the academics, we need to keep Dickens in mind, because like Dickens, King is a phenomenon—like Dickens,

King is a phenomenon in his time who at his best is also producing high-quality literature. But he also produces a lot of crap, just like Dickens produced a lot of crap. You have to separate it; you have to know how to do it. You have to be able to look at a novel like *The Shining* and hold it up against a novel like *The Dark Half* or *The Tommyknockers* and realize that there is a gap in the quality of his fiction. But when he's at his best, the books are as good as they come.

JD: If Poe and Hawthorne, both prominent writers of the Gothic, were alive today, how would they respond to King's fiction?
TM: Well, Poe would probably ask to get drunk with him or at least smoke a bowl of hash. Hawthorne might not be too receptive to his fiction. I think the people who would like King the most would be the naturalists. People like Thomas Hardy, Stephen Crane, maybe Theodore Dreiser. But certainly Hardy would have found King very interesting, because I think Hardy would have looked at his characters and recognized some of his own who are trapped by social forces, experiencing a world where we're essentially powerless very often; I'm thinking especially of *The Bachman Books*.

JD: I read Hardy's *Tess of the D'Urbervilles* just a few months ago, and I too see some common elements between that book and King's fiction—being an innocent victim, being overcome by one's evil world, everyone is susceptible to sin. And at the end of *Tess*, Tess' only refuge is in Stonehenge, an unexplained phenomenon that parallels the unexplained suffering of the human condition. I think this parallel is significant because the unexplainable become wed at the end, much like King's supernatural occurrences parallel and arise from the absurdity of an unexplainably cruel world.

Several novels now prevalent in the academics' canon deal with monsters or subhuman creatures—Shelley's *Frankenstein*, Stoker's *Dracula*, and Stevenson's *Dr. Jekyll and Mr. Hyde*. These novels receive a good deal of praise. Why is it that these books could receive applause from academics while books like *Pet Sematary*, *'Salem's Lot*, and *The Shining*, all of which deal with similar subject material as those aforementioned, would likely be ignored with a shrug?
TM: Because of what I've already said to you about the basic fact that the academic world has not read Stephen King, or if they have read books by him, the books have been dismissed, been the wrong selections, or not understood.

JD: Do you believe that King, like many other authors hailed for their greatness in literature, will not be appreciated until after he has passed away? If so, why does this tend to be the trend?

TM: I think he's plenty appreciated right now. I think whenever Stephen King decides to do something, people listen. The academic world, as perhaps is often the case, is behind the times in recognizing the need to pay attention to what this guy has to say. But that's because the academic world is a little slow. That's certainly not the case in Hollywood, for instance, where some of America's best directors have been quick to capitalize on the quality of King's work and his popular draw. You can just look at the amount of his fiction that's been turned into film—something like nineteen adaptations, many of them by America's most talented directors: Brian DePalma, David Cronenberg, Stanley Kubrick, Lewis Teague, John Carpenter, Tobe Hooper.

JD: The reason I asked that last question is because if I recall correctly, although the Romantic writers were respected when they were alive—everyone got into their writing—in most cases someone like Poe was, during his own time, like King, seen as the Great American Hack. Now, years after his death, people rave about Poe.

TM: Well, we did ignore Poe when he was alive. It was the French who recognized that Poe had tremendous talent. It took someone like Baudelaire to realize that Poe was on to something. But that's always been the case—it's taken an outsider to show us what we've got in our own culture. The same things happened with Melville and Faulkner. It took other cultures to bring our attention back to our own writers.

JD: Give me your specific list of King titles that you believe to be his greatest contributions to classic literature. Why do you think these books are worthy of inclusion in any academic's canon?

TM: I would probably go with the titles that are my favorites. I would go with *The Shining*, which strikes me as perhaps his richest text primarily because it fits into the whole concept of the Gothic haunted house and its relationship to a very critical orientation toward the social matrix that gave it birth. I would go with *It* because I think it is very much about a seminal Stephen King issue, which is the conflict between childhood and adulthood, which is something that can be traced back throughout literature and links him to the Romantic tradition, particulary Wordsworth and Dickens.

I would also include *Pet Sematary* in that list because it strikes me as perhaps the closest piece of fiction King has written to date that links to the tradition of Greek tragedy.

JD: Do you see King's work written in stages? It seems his early works were his hungriest, then, once he had established his reputation, he was able to experiment more toward the middle of his career. Now, in the latter stage of his writing, it seems he may have been taking a dip in his capabilities. The books are still enjoyable to read, I won't take that away. I guess what I'm trying to allude to is that two of his most recent books, *The Dark Half* and *Four Past Midnight*, are not as refined as some of his earlier works.
TM: Well, I think he's moving closer to splatterpunk. *The Dark Half* is a pretty good indication, and so is *Secret Window, Secret Garden* from *Four Past Midnight*, that his fiction is becoming more and more violent, gory, than it ever was. I think he's extremely restrained in books like *The Shining* or *Pet Sematary*, for instance.

JD: So you see his later works as perhaps a release of what he held back in the books you've just mentioned?
TM: Possibly. Or possibly it's a return to the excessive violence you get in *The Bachman Books*.

JD: But do you see a descent in the quality of his latest fiction?
TM: Absolutely. Because I think he's at his best when he's a hungry writer, and when he's writing fiction that reflects that hungry, autobiographical self. For instance, when he was writing *The Shining*, he was remembering rather vividly what it was like to be Stephen King three years before *Carrie*—a man living on the edge in a trailer, with wife and screaming child, a predilection toward alcohol, and some real serious misgivings about his choice of occupation.

JD: King himself has said that the first thing a good writer must do is write for himself, that you don't want to target an audience, you don't want to write to sell or use writing as a meal ticket. He feels you write for yourself, you've got to be hungry and love it, and then release it to an audience and leave it up to them whether they want it or not. I feel that King had these thoughts in mind when writing the titles you've mentioned, that all the books that have made him famous were done when he was writing for himself. How do you feel about the current $40 million contract he signed with Doubleday that obligated King to publish four books in a four-year period? Do you think that had an effect on him? I'm referring to the deadlines he had to meet because of the contract. I feel it might be possible that because of the deadlines and the money involved, King may have had to refrain from writing for himself and churn out the fiction as dictated by the agreement with his publisher.

TM: I can't answer that. I don't know what's going on in his head exactly, but I think what I'm most interested in is where Stephen King is going to go now that he's no longer hungry, now that his kids have grown up and are so clearly not an influence on him any more in the way that they were when they were so very much present in his house. One of his children is on the west coast now.

JD: One of King's recurring themes in his fiction is that adults need to keep that connection to childhood as adults. Perhaps he is now falling into the same trap that many of his fictional adult protagonists have fallen in to in the past, which is losing a firm grasp of what it is to be young?

TM: Well, clearly his orientation is changing. I think you've seen the end of Castle Rock, the end of the children. I think you're going to see more and more a writer who's having to come to terms with this absolutely phenomenal success that he's achieved, which is what *Misery* and *The Dark Half* are all about. To a certain extent, that's what *It* is about, too. In each one of those novels, the central protagonists—Bill Denbrough [*It*], Paul Sheldon [*Misery*], Thad Beaumont [*The Dark Half*]—all of these characters are all famous writers who have in some ways to come to terms with a crisis that is directly related to the phenomenon of being famous, and that's an issue that King is clearly obsessed with. You also see it in *Secret Window, Secret Garden*. This is a topic that keeps coming back for him. It's an indication of the price that you pay when you get the kind of phenomenal success he has.

JD: Although you've mentioned novels that you think lack the fundamentals of King's most powerful writing, are there any others that you would keep out of a classic canon?

TM: Oh God. I think the work that shows a lack of editing, or a lack of careful attention to detail. There are some whole sections of *Danse Macabre* that I think are absolutely brilliant, and then there are other sections that King didn't do his homework—they could use some clear, scholarly orientation and discipline. There are works of fiction that fit the same mold. I would keep out, I guess I would keep out a novel like perhaps *Cujo*, although some people are very fond of

Cujo. Certainly *Christine* is a novel that's an interesting read and it's a fun ride, but I don't think it ranks with some of his great fiction.

JD: King shows his reservations about our government often in his literature, most notably in *The Stand*, *The Dead Zone*, and *Firestarter*. Would you say underneath this attitude is a contempt for America as an institution in itself?

TM: No, I don't think so. But that's a good question because I think that at the same time King is very critical of American institutions, he's also very much involved in the whole notion of what it is to be an American. He's caught up in the idea of individuality; if you look at the survivors in King's fiction, as I talk about in my own book, they are always characters who form small-group relationships who are at the heart of the whole notion of the American experience: the individual separating him- or herself from the mainstream. If King is anti-patriotic or anti-American, he's no more so than was Thoreau before him, or Mark Twain, or Melville, or Emerson, and these are the gods of American literature.

JD: Why does King's fiction demand recognition beyond its entertainment value?

TM: Because I think his fiction can teach us a lot about ourselves, it can teach us a lot about the society we share. It's one of the reasons why he's one of the most popular writers in the world right now. Because American culture is one of the most popular cultures in the world right now. I was in Italy about ten years ago, and there are more American studies, American literature majors, at the University of Milan than there are at the University of Vermont. It's just a thing that draws people; we're an interesting country, and the world likes to talk about us, for better or for worse.

II. **Carroll Terrell**, retired English professor, University of Maine at Orono. Terrell taught King when King was a college student at UMO. He had regular interaction with King as a student when King was in his pre-published years, viewing drafts of King's first full-length manuscripts and giving guidance concerning the continuance of his writing. He still has contact with him on an infrequent basis. Terrell has published books criticizing Louis Zukofsky, Basil Bunting, William Carlos Williams, and Ezra Pound. His most recent publications are a book on King called *Stephen King: Man and Artist* (Northern Lights, 1990) and *Ideas in Reaction: Byways to the Pound Arcana* (Northern Lights, 1991).

This interview was conducted orally in July, 1991.

JD: Tell me your career association with UMO.
CT: Well, I came here in 1948 for a summer session. I guess it was a national emergency and they didn't have anybody to teach so they hired me to stay. The only question they asked was "Can you walk?" I could walk, and so I started teaching here. I had been planning to have a job in Washington, but I stayed on and on and on and never left.

JD: What year did you decide to retire?
CT: 1982.

JD: Where did you complete your education?
CT: I got my Ph.D. from New York University.

JD: Please describe to me the first time you met Stephen King and the impression he made on you.
CT: The fall of 1967. I was sitting at my desk, I looked up, and there was this tall, gangly fellow standing there—stalkly-looking fella with steel-gray eyes. He said, "Burt Hatlen said I should show you this." I thought it might be an M.A. thesis. I thought he was a bit young for an M.A., but then students were getting younger all the time from my point of view. And so I said, "What is it?" He said, "It's a novel. I wrote it." "Oh," I said. So I took it home and read it that night, with dawning amazement. He was a sophomore, and that one so young could write a novel seemed unlikely. It was called "The Long Walk."

It had a beginning, a middle, and an end. It was all there, and no sophomore should be able to write with such design.

JD: Did King excel in his curriculum? Was he a student who shone above others?

CT: No. In classes he had with me, he did A's, on tests and things like that. With the system at the time, I had a hundred students in the class, and I refused to have more than that. He was in the back there somewhere most of the time, but there was no dialogue. Nobody was really a participant. I would say "Are there any questions?" And the whole of them would just sit there and not ask anything. And if they did, they learned not to. As one fella said, "You must never ask him a question, because if you do, he's very likely to answer it and then you'll be sorry." Because I'd go on and on and on and then end up asking, "What was the question?"

JD: Did King strike you as the type who would pursue the career that has made him perhaps the most-recognized author of modern times? Did such thoughts even cross your mind?

CT: Oh, I didn't think he was going to be what he is. Nobody would think such a thing. He's a natural writer, and at the time when I was teaching him, I had finished reading "The Long Walk," and he had come in to talk about it. It was kind of sad because he wanted to know if it could be published. I didn't think there was a nickel's worth a chance, the publishing world being what it is. It was a parable, nothing to do with the real world. It didn't have anything to do with anything going on in the world at the time. He thought that was pretty dismissible, that I didn't know what I was talking about. I don't remember exactly now, but I think I said, "Your chances of being published would be better if you did something topical, something that's going on now. Something that matters most in the country." That was during the Vietnam war, you know. There were student reactions on campuses all over the country against the war. So he started to do another book. He got halfway through it, he'd come in, and we'd talk about it.

But you see, he's a natural writer. Anybody who goes ordinarily and takes creative-writing courses, they think writing has to do with sentences. It has nothing to do with it. So anyway, we'd talk about the new book, he'd go write some more. I remember he said when it was halfway through, "Do you think the publishers would give me an advance?" I didn't think he needed any money at the time, I didn't know. I don't know how he did all he did, working through college, doing all of his writing, taking all of these courses. I said that he could send it, but that what they would tell him would be that they couldn't give him an advance, but they'd like to read the rest of it. So one day he dropped in with a letter from the publisher and he said, "At least you hit that nail on the head." He never did publish it. It was called "Sword in the Darkness."

JD: Tell me what kind of a personal individual King was as a college-aged young man.
CT: I only got to know him from when he came to the office to talk about his writing. He was working things out where he was going to write and be a teacher. I told him that was a mistake. A lot of people do that: they think they want to be writers so they think that's the thing to do—teach high school English. Well, in fact that would give you less time. Eighty hours a week just doesn't do it. If you're going to teach something, teach elementary school grades, and do it in a certain way so that if you leave the office, you leave the school at three o'clock and think nothing more about it. It's all about management of time.

JD: Do you feel King's growing up in Maine and his choice to stay there has shaped his success?
CT: He's a writer and it wouldn't make any difference where he grew up. He'd be a writer, and that's that. No, it's had nothing to do with his success. Obviously the places he's known and seen and the people he's more familiar with influence what he does, but he could have grown up among the Hopi Indians and he still would have been a writer. For that matter, if he'd grown up in Alaska, it'd still have nothing to do with it.

JD: Why do you suppose King chose to remain in Bangor rather than move out to Los Angeles or New York where the hearts of the industry lie?
CT: Well, I'll tell you what. It's because he's got brains, that's why. My object in life is one thing only: my desire in the end is never to have to cross the Stillwater River [note: the Stillwater surrounds the UMO campus]. What he did was logical [live temporarily in other locations], and he did it in likable places. He did just like any reasonable person would do who comes to Maine: go looking all over. I was in the Army for five years and saw all kinds of places. All that does is prove to you that the best place to be is in Maine. Peru, Ecuador, France—blah, who wants to live in such horrible places. He

lived in England for a while, thought he was going to stay there. He didn't even stay as long as he planned. He went there for three or four months and said the hell with it, came back here. I mean, how are you going to deal with such unreasonable...I take that back. How are you going to deal with such PEOPLE? You go out, you watch, and then you get back home again.

Where do you come from?

JD: I come from near Chicago.
CT: Chicago. Well there's an unreasonable place.

JD: It seems that a group evolving as an academic elite has sculpted a canon of acceptable literature that is essential to any English program. As an English professor, tell me what qualities go into classic writing. In other words, what makes a particular work of fiction great?
CT: The answer to that question would take you two books. What makes a book great? Vitality. Perception. Ability to get down on the page just what these people are up to and why. As far as King is concerned, the only thing that matters is the story, which is what matters most. The rest after that is detail. It matters if people are interested in reading it. One time we were talking, and King said to me, "It's all very easy. It's like a fisherman: you drop the hook in the water and you get the fish to nibble and bite. They bite and you set the hook. You get the hook set well enough and then you can play with them all you want and they can't get away." That's all there is to writing a great novel.

How do you get into the canon? There's always a great fight in academia about what should be in and what should not be in. All of this takes place, and it doesn't have very much meaning in the long run. People are going to read what they want to read; they're quite independent of what professors say is in the canon. People go on what is being said and done at the moment.

There was a time, and I'll tell you exactly when it was: 1919. That was the history of the birth of Herman Melville. If you studied before that in literature, in colleges it was English literature. There was no such thing as American literature. So they said to themselves, "Well, we're important now. We're going to have to have American literature." They dug up *Moby Dick* because that was the hundredth year from Melville's birthday. They promoted that as the Great American Novel. And then they dug around and found some other stuff. And then they were all looking around to find what were going to be the great ones now. They got F. Scott Fitzgerald, Hemingway, and all these people who come and go to be the great ones.

JD: King obviously has been for the most part excluded from the canon as far as the college classroom goes. Should he be included?
CT: Certainly not. What difference? It doesn't make any difference. What they do there doesn't do any particular damage in the long run, but it doesn't do any good, either. It doesn't have very much to do with anything. They're mostly concerned with criticism, deconstruction; they talk to each other for promotion and pay or some damn thing. It doesn't have to do with real life as I know. And there are professors who have never read King. They say "That nonsense?" or "That bullshit? Hell, no." And I say "Well, which book do you mean?" And it turns out they haven't read anything.

Academia does determine the canon for the moment, but it's always being changed.

JD: Professor Tony Magistrale from the University of Vermont quoted another scholar, Leslie Fiedler, in saying that fifty years from now, King's literature will be looked at as an accurate barometer of the eighties and nineties. Do you agree with this prediction?
CT: Ah, I would say yes, the human condition at the moment.

JD: During my second day in Maine, I visited the King home twice. Both times I was not alone. Other people were either driving by slowly or standing with me in front of the house. The first person I met, a woman from Boston, appeared to me to be a King fanatic. She confided in me that she had every King novel in hardback and that she would let no one touch them. It is highly obvious that King has tripped some live wire in the American public that has created some profound effects. What do you think King appeals to in his reading public?
CT: I don't know. I don't know, for instance, why people go crazy about anybody. Prince. Michael Jackson. The Beatles, which was when I remember the first time this magnetism taking place. I don't know. It's very curious, a manifestation of something or other.

JD: Well, take away the fanaticism, why are King's readers, on a level of respect and appreciation outside of being fanatics, so drawn to his works?
CT: His power of getting people on the page. There's more to it than that: it's his rhythm, his knowing what to put in and what not to put in.

JD: Do you yourself see King as a literary force to be reckoned with? If so, why? Elaborate on your feelings about the content of his fiction.

CT: He's concerned with the human condition, where it came from, and where it's going. I think any great writer has to. I look at him as a baseball player in left field who sees the ball in the air and knows where he's going to have to be in order to catch it. He's concerned with social problems, of course. The poisoned planet. The ridiculousness of the United States government. There are 250 million people in the United States, one percent of that is 2.5 million. It's ridiculous that most of the crime and everything you read in the newspapers is committed or caused by that one percent. And it's a crime that most of them have to be senators, doctors, educated people who should know better. They sell the United States and everything in it down the river to be re-elected. They're up to it now. And then they have secret government components like King's The Shop [in *Firestarter*]. They'll go out and shoot anybody all over the world if necessary. So King's the kind of writer to say "What would happen if...?"

JD: Do you look at King as being the same type of contributor to twentieth-century American literature as say someone like William Faulkner or Flannery O'Connor? Does King have his place in this century?

CT: Oh yes. As far as I'm concerned, in the twentieth century in America, Faulkner is the only one that has a canvas that approaches King's.

JD: Do you see parallels between King and Mark Twain? They both have a very strong sense of a journey across physical space that correlates with their own moral and spiritual development. In *Huckleberry Finn*, the relationship between Huck and Nigger Jim could be seen as a parallel of the relationship between Jack Sawyer and Speedy Parker in *The Talisman*. Both relationships have a bond between a young white boy and an older black man who is primitive by the way adult white men see him. The bond they form together allows them to separate from the larger mechanism of society that operates to suppress them, who are both in subordinated positions— child and racial minority.

CT: Oh, yes. One of the great lines in *Huck Finn* is "All right. I'll go to hell." He's going to stick with Jim no matter what, and he'll go to hell if that's what he has to do. He won't turn him in.

One of the most potent things in King's work is a statement in...I think it's from *The Bachman Books*, where he talks about the trained-dog ethic. Now you better listen to this you see, because if you get the right idea through your thick head you'll find it will change your life! Did you know you were conditioned, brainwashed, from birth to the present moment by that thing [points at a newspaper], everything there is out there? Here it is: [quoting from his own book, which he holds in his hand] "Let us take the energy crisis as an example. The American people are the trained dogs—trained in this case to love oil-guzzling toys, cars, snowmobiles, large boats, dune buggies, motorcycles, mini-cycles, campers, and many, many more. In the years 1973 to 1980, we will be trained to hate energy toys. The American people love to be trained. Training makes them wag their tails—Use energy! Don't use energy! Go pee on the newspaper! (Are you ready?) I don't object to saving energy, I object to the training." This is like Pavlov's dog. But finally, a conclusion which is thematic. We're all King's dogs at work. We were trained to salivate at the bell. We've been trained to salivate when somebody shows us a list of gadgets we should have. I've left something out the conclusion of this: "It isn't the trained-dog ethic that I object to, anyway. It's the fact that the masters are mental, moral, and spiritual idiots." So, what chance do you have? You haven't got much of a chance because you've been trained in schools, churches, that thing [points at newspaper], advertising, everything else by a bunch of mental, moral, and spiritual idiots. All of King's work explores that and shows how it's true.

JD: King is a very accessible writer; people can read his books without a great deal of trouble with the narrative. Do you suppose this is why he has been slammed by academia?

CT: He uses the language of the people. He does exactly what the great writers of the past have done with that choice. Shakespeare, in his own time, was looked down upon by professors at Oxford and Cambridge; they wouldn't go see one of his plays, unless they were slumming. He used the language of the people. Shakespeare uses more one-syllable words than any writer in history. You take any Shakespeare piece written in iambic pentameter, and count the number of lines that have ten or eleven words in it. He not only uses one-syllable words, he uses words with the least letters in them. When he has to deal with life and death, he says, "To be or not to be." Jesus, you give that to an Oxford professor, I don't know what he'd make of it.

That was also the choice Dante made. There was a literary language in Italy at the time, and all Dante did was choose the dialect of the people as spoken, the Tuscan dialect. Only a few scholars took him seriously.

JD: Do you feel that like the fates of many now-termed great authors, King's appreciation as a powerful artist of fiction from an academic's point of view will not be heightened until after he has passed away?

CT: Well, I think that's the irony. That is, the popular fiction of one age becomes the classic fiction of the next. The function of the future will take care of itself. What the people want in the end will prevail, and it doesn't have anything to do with what they do or don't do at Yale, Harvard or any other place. And my impression is that the support of the following he has is based on only one thing: THEY WANT TO READ HIS BOOKS. You ask them why, they won't know. Because THEY LIKE TO READ HIS BOOKS.

JD: Of everything King has written, which works of his fiction do you think represent the artist he truly is? Why?

CT: *The Stand. It. The Body.* Because he's there; he understands kids while their elders don't. Adults are the real monsters. You can't tell them anything: they won't understand. You go ask them something, and they say, "I understand perfectly well. I was once your age." So all the kids can do is go BLAH, and pretty soon they won't tell them anything. In *It*, you think those kids are going to tell their parents anything? No, hell no. They won't know anything about it. They'll say "You're all imagining it." So they're on their own.

Well, kids start reading King in grammar school, some of them. And in the high schools, because at least Big King understands. He understands the language, he understands what they say, understands their problems and everything else.

JD: What works do you see as being below their potential? Why?

CT: Well, I call them 'fun diversions.' Some of these horror things, shock stories, are fun diversions that have nothing to do with his serious work; they're another category. Some of the short stories about space things and so forth, but they have a point behind them. I like to read them all; they're interesting. But when you've written as many as he has, you're bound to have some falling off at some points.

You see, I agree with the themes so much; I agree with everything he's getting at.

JD: How do you view King's feelings about God?
CT: He believes in God unpersonified. Ezra Pound calls it the "intimate essence." You see, there's no way you can communicate with people on the subject because if you use a word such as 'God,' that will evoke in the mind of the reader everything they've read about it or think about it. So you can't even use it. Pound's idea, which is the same as mine or King's or any other reasonable person, is that God is invented: the image of the old white-bearded Satan, as Pound refers to it, sitting somewhere in outer space.

JD: King has a tremendous tendency to punish moral corruption at both the personal and institutional levels in his fiction. One of his most recurring themes is a self-serving American government that leaves U.S. citizens expendable for the sake of making the governmental machine more powerful than it already is. Is King pessimistic toward America? I read once that prior to Vietnam, King's reservations about the government were not as strong as they have been since after the war.
CT: Yes, he is. He looks around, as far as I can see, for some sign, but he doesn't see any. He sees everybody in the Congress has been bought by something for political reasons. They've decided they need to keep on spending $30 billion of the budget for the CIA. What the hell is the CIA going to do with $30 billion? During the Cold War it might have made sense, but now. Wow, it's ridiculous.

JD: What do you see as King's optimism, his key to salvation? What hope does he offer for survival in this world?
CT: Well, it's in the common man, but I think he has less hope than I do. I don't know the answer to that. I think that independent of what people either do or don't do in the long run, the divine spirit will prevail, and that's all there is to that.

JD: You've already mentioned that you would not favor the introduction of King's fiction into the classroom. However, if the idea were being entertained by academics, and you were called upon to stand before a board of English professors representing a high council of the U.S. English curriculum that was about to cast its final verdict, what would your defense of King be?

CT: Well, my defense is that he is an artist of extraordinary power. He has the ability to see the human condition, how it's evolved in the last four hundred years to the point it is now, and what we have to look forward to. He can do it with considerably more talent, skill, power, and knowledge than anybody else.

III. **Burton Hatlen,** University of Maine at Orono. Hatlen, an English professor, taught King when King was a student at UMO. After taking Hatlen's class in Hatlen's first semester at UMO, King continued to correspond with him both in and out of the classroom. Even to this day, Hatlen and King communicate and get together once or twice a year to talk or enjoy a movie. Hatlen played a major role in guiding a young King in his writing endeavors and was also one of three recipients of the dedication to King's *The Long Walk*, a Bachman Book. He has contributed fine essays on several occasions to collections of King criticism. His most recent is "Good and Evil in Stephen King's *The Shining*," which can be found in Tony Magistrale's *"The Shining"* Reader (Starmont House, 1990).

This interview was conducted orally in July, 1991.

JD: Tell me the extent of your involvement with UMO.

BH: Well, I've been teaching here since 1967, so it's sort of my life. I started as an assistant professor, and now I'm a full professor. I was the department chairman for three years—1985 to 1988. I teach all sorts of different stuff, but my official specialty is Renaissance English literature. I teach a good deal of modern literature, too, and creative writing.

JD: I've been reading "King's Garbage Truck", the newspaper column he wrote when he was a student here, and he had credited you as being a pretty open-minded poetry reader, too.

BH: Well, I don't remember the column, but it's nice to know it's in there. I was involved with a poetry workshop that met during his student years here and involved both faculty and students. He was probably referring to that. We met every week it seems to me for a period of several months. What we did was bring in poetry and my job actually with the workshop was to xerox material and distribute it. He was a very active member of that, as was Tabitha [his wife]. That's part of my background with him, and that's probably what he was thinking about in that column.

JD: Describe to me the first time you met King and the immediate impression he made on you.

BH: He was a student in a class that I taught during my first semester here. I came in 1967, and in September of that year I started teaching a class on modern American literature, which was a bit of a surprise because my specialty was Renaissance literature, but they needed somebody to teach the class, and I had done a master's degree on William Carlos Williams, the twentieth-century poet. So I had a reasonable amount of background with twentieth-century literature. I was asked to teach the class, and he took the course. It was a large class—I think there were fifty or sixty students in it. I became aware of him as a student in the class because he was a very faithful student, he looked interested, he asked smart questions in class, he said intelligent things about the stuff we were reading. Several weeks into the semester he came up to me after class one day and said, "I've written a novel. Would you be willing to read it?" I said yes. It was the manuscript of *The Long Walk*. I was very impressed by this; it was clear that here was a natural writer. So I was very much aware of him from that point on, although I do remember sort of visual images of him in class before then.

JD: Did you and King share a close relationship when you were teaching him during his years at UMO? Were you friends outside of the classroom?

BH: Well, yes. After that first class he took from me, during that year, another teacher and I planned a class for the following year on contemporary American poetry. I was writing poetry, interested in it, and a new program was started by the College of Arts and Sciences called Special Seminars, which could be courses outside the normal curriculum. Jim Bishop, the other teacher, and I, planned the course on contemporary American poetry. Steve took that class. It was a group of about twelve students, I believe. That class became a real catalyst for creating a kind of community that lasted really for the next three years or so; that is, several people came together in that class who were heavily engaged with writing, especially poetry. A poetry workshop, the one I mentioned previously, grew out of that class.

The year I met him would have been his sophomore year. He was starting his sophomore year at that time. The year of the special seminar on contemporary American poetry was his junior year, so I saw a lot of him in the class, and then the workshop extended beyond that class through the rest of that year. The workshop, in my recollection, continued on through the next fall also. I saw a good deal of him outside of that context, too. I remember being at parties with him. He would come by my office rather frequently, and we would talk about writing, life, and stuff like this. So yeah, I would say I saw a good deal of him, although I'm sure that he was more involved with students, and that he had a circle of student friends he saw a good deal of. But I have a lot of memories of meetings with him as long as he was a student here.

JD: From what I've learned in all of my research on him and from reading "King's Garbage Truck" and Doug Winter's book on him, it seems as though he was a pretty unique, eccentric guy. I guess he really pulled himself up—he wasn't exactly the wealthiest kid in the world. He had to work hard during college for money, and until he wrote *Carrie*, he was always in a financial bind. He got food on the table, but he was never really comfortable. Did you also see something extraordinarily eccentric about him when you were dealing with him?

BH: Well, he was certainly a very powerful presence. Yeah, he was poor. He was working all through college. One incident I remember quite vividly was I think probably at the beginning of his junior year or perhaps during his senior year. He came by my office and said that for one reason or another he had not turned in his financial aid application on time, and they had told him that because he was late with the application, they weren't going to give him any financial aid for the next year. He was very distressed about this and said he wouldn't be able to come back to school if he couldn't get financial aid. He asked me if I could do anything, and I said yeah, I'd see what I could do. I went to the financial aid office and said that here was a remarkably unusual student and you really should do what you can to keep him here. And they did waive the requirement and gave him financial aid. That's a sign of how little money he had.

It was clear he was really poor, both from clothes and things like that. But he was also in retrospect an extremely forceful personality. The sheer number of things that he did—here you have a student who was dependent on financial aid and on working part-time. He was working in the library most of the time. He had a column in the student newspaper, was a member of student government, a very active member of the student senate, he wrote at least two or three hours every day, he read an average of a book a day. He had an active social life. He acted in plays in the theater program here. He was politically active—he participated in demonstrations and things like this. I just don't know how he had the time to do all of it when I think back on it. Virtually everybody who was here in those years remembers him as a presence on the campus. Of course he was visually quite astounding. I don't know if you've ever seen the picture that was taken of him that appeared on the cover of the student newspaper. They devoted the whole front page to this picture. He's got hair down to his shoulders, this scraggly beard. It was about the time of the movie *Deliverance*. It was sort of a take-off on that. He's got a shotgun aimed right into the camera lens so that you see the double barrels of the shotgun right there. And these wild eyes are just staring at you. Underneath, the caption was "STUDY, DAMN IT!" He's got a blow-up of this on the wall of his home. That picture has been pulled out and used in various ways over the years. If you saw him then, you remembered him.

JD: You already said you were impressed by the first novel he brought in for you to read. But besides that first impression, did you see him becoming what he is today?

BH: Well, I certainly saw him as a writer. The other person who I talked with was Ted Holmes, who was a creative writing teacher here then. He's still around here [note: Ted Holmes and Jim Bishop are the two other recipients of the dedication to *The Long Walk*]. I do remember meeting him in the hallway shortly after he had read the manuscript, and I remember him saying, "I think we have a real writer." So he was getting recognition of that sort. Ted, who's a short story writer—he has published three books of short stories—had an agent in New York at the time. He sent *The Long Walk* to his agent at Steve's request. The agent read it and said that she thought the interest was too local—that it would be interesting to Maine people but not to others. She turned it down. I think that was Steve's first real attempt to publish a novel.

I thought *The Long Walk* was a spectacular performance. My tastes then and now are not primarily oriented toward popular literature, although one of the things that my relationship with Steve has done is lead me to read stuff that I would not otherwise have read. So, knowing him has changed my life in some significant ways. I've published articles on *Dracula*, for example, which I read because I read *'Salem's Lot*, which Steve said was a take-off on *Dracula*. I was not a reader of science fiction at the time I read *The Long Walk*. What I did respond to I think was simply the intensity of the narrative pace. Here was somebody who really knew how to tell a story, that grabbed you and kept you going. And that seems to me almost instinct. I don't know that that's something that can be taught, and he clearly had it.

JD: It is apparent that he was and is someone who could never stop working.

BH: He still reads a lot. Another sign of what an unusual student he was—a story I've told frequently, but it does seem to me kind of typical—was the Special Seminar program where we did the course on contemporary American poetry during his junior year. During his senior year, he decided that he wanted to teach a course in this program on popular fiction. He felt that the curriculum of the English department tended to be snobbish, elitist, and oriented toward old stuff. He thought there should be a course here on popular fiction, and nobody in the department was really in a position to teach it, so he said, "Well, why don't I teach it?" He took this proposal to a committee that reviewed proposals for the special seminars. He took the proposal in, and the committee reviewed it and said, yeah, it sounds like a fine idea, but we can't have an undergraduate teaching a credit course in a university, it's just unheard of. So he recruited another faculty member, a man named Graham Adams, who was also part of the poetry workshop group, not as centrally involved as Jim Bishop or I was but he used to come regularly and wrote some poetry. Graham agreed to be the front person for it. He did all the paperwork and signed the grade sheets at the end of the course. But Steve actually taught the course. And I would guess that's still the only time in the history of this university that an undergraduate has actually taught a course. What he did was teach the kind of stuff that he was interested in—Shirley Jackson, Lovecraft, Poe.

JD: Are you yourself an avid King fan?

BH: I try to read just about everything. I'm usually a year or so behind. I'm reading the latest book of short novels—*Four Past Midnight.*

JD: Were there or have there been other students who you would have thought would have succeeded before King did? Why did King succeed?

BH: I think he did shine. It was clear he knew what he wanted to do. He knew he wanted to be a writer, and he knew exactly what kind of writer he wanted to be. He was already working on becoming that, and that's very unusual. I was never surprised that he made it, though I was surprised that he made it quite so...spectacularly.

JD: It's got to be quite an experience to have been involved with him for so many years before this happened, and then to have been a friend and confidante of his and watch him become this worldwide smash. I think everyone in America knows who he is.

BH: It's an odd experience in many ways because he's still in some ways this KID that I knew, you know. I mean, I can still sort of see him in those terms, and I then I realize that other people can't or don't.

Last fall, *It* was on television—the two-part series. He's known that I'm a particular fan of that book, which I do like a lot, although I do think it's imperfect in certain ways. But especially the adolescent sections where he's writing about the kids has really some of the very best writing he's ever done. He called me up and asked if I wanted to come over and watch it. I did. When the credits came on: STEPHEN KING'S "IT," you know, he said you couldn't imagine how peculiar it feels to have your name sort of, well, this wasn't his comparison, but sort of like IVORY SOAP or something.

Years ago, he wrote a piece called "On Becoming a Brand Name." When he wrote that, he had scarcely begun to become a real brand name. Now he is, and yet there's a person connected with this name; the media tends to simply cancel out the person and turn you into pure image. It's peculiar; he feels it's peculiar. I just can't comprehend it. I think of him as somebody I know. I'm also aware that there's this kind of mass-recognition phenomenon. But I just don't find any way of moving back and forth between the two. So it's become more and more difficult for me to deal with the question of talking about him for that reason. Last fall, the FOX TV network was going to do a show on him and came through here. They wanted to do an interview and I said okay. They taped an hour interview with me. They were trying to get me to give away things; they wanted something scandalous, something really hot, that they could use. I found that experience so unpleasant that I decided I would not do any more public interviews on him. The problem is these media people have no recognition, respect, of the personal dimension of the relationship; it's all glitz, as far as they're concerned. He refused to see them. In retrospect, I'm glad he did.

JD: Do you feel growing up in Maine had a profound impact on King as an artist that would not have been there had he grown up near Chicago, New York, Los Angeles or the rural South? If he had grown up near these other places, what kind of writer would he have been, or better yet, would he have been a writer at all?

BH: You should realize he did not grow up entirely in Maine. The landscape in *It*, for example, is a mixture of Bangor and the town in

Pennsylvania where he lived. So those out-of-state experiences were very important to him. He's clearly got a strong sense of loyalty to the state, and part of it is that this is his turf as a writer.

One thing I might mention: in that course in modern American literature that he took from me, we read both Steinbeck and Faulkner. Both are writers that have had a strong impact on him; he continues to read both of them. What he saw in both of them was a regional kind of focus. Although he's obviously set books elsewhere than in Maine, I think he feels most comfortable here. He feels that he knows the state, he knows the feel of life here. So even in a book like *The Stand*, where he has the characters sort of moving out, he has significant sections of it set in Maine.

I think Maine was good for him in a lot of ways. I think he himself blows hot and cold about the university, but mostly I think this was a very good place for him to be a student. I think he got a lot of recognition here, and he got fewer put-downs for the kind of literary interests that he was pursuing; he got fewer of those here than he would have gotten in most other places. Any academic institution is liable to go on a model of great literature as separated from trash. He was deliberately playing off of the trash idea; you can see that in "King's Garbage Truck." Where do you think he got the title from? He's hauling out the trash. But this is a relatively unpretentious place, and I think that was the right place for him to be. I would say he also had very good experiences in high school. He apparently had a teacher who really saw him as remarkably promising, and he keeps putting these high-school English teachers into novels because he did have this good experience with them, and he himself wanted to be a high school teacher because of the response that he got as a student.

One thing that's important to remember about him is that he was a fatherless kid. He did tend to sort of focus on father surrogates. I think the most important one—I never met the man—was the high school teacher who was the model for the teacher in *'Salem's Lot*, Matt Burke. That character is based on a real person. I also think Maine has been a good place for him to live as an adult writer because he can live in Bangor most of the time and lead a relatively normal life. People do leave him alone. The Maine people will leave you alone; that's a big advantage of life in this state. This recent incident with the guy breaking into the house is the first time something like this has happened. It's a very disturbing event because I'm afraid it will lead them [the Kings] to feel they can't lead a normal life here, and that would be a real shame if that should happen.

JD: As an English student who had attended three different colleges, I have come across at least two dozen different English instructors. I'd say all but two regarded King as pop-culture junk. I have come to believe that an academic elite has emerged that invests the power in itself to dictate what is classic literature worthy of inclusion in the classroom. In your own words, what makes a piece of fiction classic, and, collectively, what makes a writer classic?

BH: Well, I'm going to mostly avoid that question. It certainly is true that there is that kind of...the usual code word for it these days is 'canonization.' That is, there is a literary canon. The classics, and then there's mass culture, popular culture, etc., everything that's sort of outside the canon. And most academics tend to think in terms of either/ors in this respect. However, that's a situation that has broken down, is breaking down, quite rapidly. There's a lot of interest in popular culture in the academic world. And I'm interested, for instance, in the Modern Language Association's bibliography of scholarship on everybody.

JD: They have stuff on Stephen King in there?

BH: Yeah. [He grabs two green volumes]. This is the latest one; I haven't checked on it. [He flips through the pages]. Only two items here in the 1989 volume. Here's 1988. There are seven items on Steve here. So he's getting recognition. It's a relatively slow process, but I think that the kinds of oppositions that you're talking about there are tending to break down. Younger faculty tend not to think in those terms.

JD: You've already mentioned that he's starting to get more recognition, but do you think he should be in the same class as say someone like Faulkner? Years from now, will Stephen King be the William Shakespeare, the William Faulkner?

BH: Again I'm going to evade that one because...let's take the case of William Faulkner, for instance. There's a recent book on Faulkner which is about how Faulkner was established as a major writer. It's about the politics of literary canonization. The argument of the book is that in the years right after World War II, partly for reasons of cultural nationalism, there was a feeling that the U.S. needed a great writer. In a lot of ways, Faulkner was picked out by these powerful literary critics who had Southern connections—Robert Penn Warren, Alan Tate. There was a group of literary critics who had zeroed in on Faulkner as THE ONE. There was a convergence between what they did and some interest in Faulkner from France in particular. This is not to say that you can arbitrarily decide you're going to establish so-and-so as a major writer and begin a political campaign to do it. I think that Faulkner is a very interesting, powerful writer. I also think that—and I'm speaking now from Steve's point of view—Steve might say at this point that John Steinbeck is also a very powerful, compelling writer. Steinbeck did not get canonized in the way that Faulkner did. If you look in the MLA bibliography at this point in time, [he flips open a volume again], this is a quickie lesson in literary politics, here's Faulkner: just numbers of items. There are fifteen items on this page, and pieces on him fill up the next two whole pages. We'll compare this to Steinbeck. Just a few items. He's not gone, but he has nothing compared to Faulkner.

One of the things that happens is that scholarly attention and criticism breed more of the same. That is, as more gets written about Faulkner you get a self-perpetuating process. The mistake is to assume that somehow these patterns reflect some objective truth about the literary value of the stuff we're talking about, that Faulkner must be eight times as great a writer as Steinbeck because he's got eight times more attention in here [points at the volume].

On Steve, what I would say is this. From the beginning, he set himself a goal of trying to bridge the gap between traditional, serious literature and mass culture. He didn't want to accept the limitations of either one. This was a really remarkable decision for him to make about himself as a writer. I wouldn't say he's the only person to try to bridge that gap by any means. Steinbeck did; Hemingway did. King did it somewhat differently in that he deliberately went after certain genres which had never been really effectively reconciled with the notion of high literature. That is, the notion that serious literature was in a realistic mode got established in the nineteenth century, and it has tended to dominate discussions of fiction throughout the twentieth century. Serious literature was in the realistic mode, and if you were writing science fiction, fantasy, etc., you were writing extra-literary fiction.

When he was a student, those dichotomies were starting to break down, partly because of Tolkien. Tolkien was an important influence. He hasn't talked very much about Tolkien. But he's told me *The Stand* was quite consciously based on *The Lord of the Rings*. Tolkien managed to be taken seriously by literary scholars and be vastly popular for a period in the 1960s and 1970s, and Tolkien was writing fantasy. So here it became possible once again to look at fantasy as serious, real literature. But in the meantime, Steve has also looked to writers who work in best-seller, mass-culture kinds of modes. Most such writing is formulaic. If you read one Robert Ludlum novel, you basically know the formula for any other Ludlum novel. Detective stories are formulaic, and science fiction is essentially formulaic. What Steve did that makes him different from most genre writers is he never established a formula and then just to rework it. If you compare him to other people who have had enormously successful careers as best-selling writers in the last thirty years— Jacqueline Susann, Ludlum, Danielle Steele, Tom Clancy—all of them, and I don't do more than sample these people, but my sense is that they're all basically formula writers. Steve is not that. That seems to me a major difference. He's been rethinking the mode in every book that he's done up to *The Tommyknockers*; the first one where that seemed not to be happening in my judgment was *The Tommyknockers*. That he doesn't repeat himself augers well for his future within the world of literature. In *Fear Itself*, he compares himself to Dickens, and that seems to me to be a very useful and valuable comparison because Dickens was also enormously popular, but he was also rethinking the form in all of his novels. The other writer that Steve has compared himself to at times, and again I think it's a useful comparison, is Jack London. I think that the role that Steve has played in American culture is very similar in many ways to the role that Jack London played. London is an odd figure in American literature because he never really made it into the American literature canon, although in other countries, he's seen as one of our major writers.

JD: Are there any other writers aside from the ones you've mentioned that you saw as having a significant influence on King?
BH: Shirley Jackson is the other writer that you should keep in mind. He admired her greatly. When he was here as a student, he was much under the influence of both the kind of social sense that you get in a story like "The Lottery" and the really classic sort of horror novel that you get in *The Haunting of Hill House*. I think he learned a lot from her. And I think there's been a sense in his work from the beginning that New England was kind of Gothic turf here. *Dark Shadows* is another thing you ought to take a look at if you're really looking at the sources because he was watching that show in the 1960s. That's supposedly set somewhere on the Maine coast. H.P. Lovecraft was another—a very important influence. I think he's read and reread Lovecraft over and over. Lovecraft is a regional writer, too, also New England—Providence, Rhode Island.

JD: I'd like to tell you a story that I've presented in other interviews. I went to King's house on my second day here in Maine, and I noticed immediately the huge attraction King's home has in Bangor. The first person I met, a woman from Boston, was standing with me in front of the house. She said she was glad I was there so that she wouldn't look like the only lunatic milling in front of a celebrity's home. She explained to me that she had every Stephen King book in hard cover and that she would let no one touch them. When I told her what I was doing in Maine, she became ecstatic. She wanted me to let him know that she had stopped by should I get the chance to meet him. It seems King through the power of his written word has tapped into some internal wire that sets off a reaction in his public. Why does he have this power?

BH: Part of it is this kind of star mentality, and I would discount some of it in that respect. He produces this Elvis Presley kind of image. However, I also think that the audience is quite a distinctive one in that a lot of people who don't read books read a Stephen King novel and said "Wow, this really speaks to me in some way." And the involvement is partly just a response to his storytelling abilities—his ability to get his hooks in you as a writer, and you just need to keep going; you need to know what's going to happen next here. He has a very compelling narrative sense, as strong a narrative sense as any writer who's ever lived.

He once said to me something that seemed to me really to sum up what he's all about as a writer. He said "A writer like Flaubert in *Madame Bovary* writes about extraordinary people in ordinary circumstances. I write about ordinary people in extraordinary circumstances." And I think that has a lot to do with people reading these books and finding individuals in them that they identify with without any real leap of the imagination. He takes ordinary people seriously. *The Stand* is a novel that I think in a very spectacular way attests to what I'm saying here: that the guy who pumps the gas in your corner service station is potentially a kind of heroic figure. If you spend any time with Steve, one of the things that's really striking to me about him is that I think he really does have that kind of relationship with people, which makes it too bad that he's in a sense a star and therefore can't engage with people in an ordinary, everyday way. And this is one reason that he's kind of ambivalent about the university. He would really rather hang out with the janitors; actually when he taught here, that's what he tended to do. To most academics, they're just these people who come around and empty your wastebaskets; you don't pay much attention to them. But he did. He just likes to find out what's going on with people like that. And actually I think that at this stage in his life, he probably still does do a fair amount of this because often these people don't know who he is, and he can just get into a conversation with somebody behind the counter at the local 7-Eleven and get some sense of his/her life. He takes ordinary people with absolute seriousness.

JD: What works would you say best represent the artist that he truly is?

BH: I'm a long-time admirer of *'Salem's Lot*. I've read it several times; I think it holds up very well. I think that's the first book where he really hit it all. He was sort of humming. I like *The Stand* a lot. *The Stand* seems to me aesthetically in some ways less controlled.

In the early days I used to read the stuff in manuscript before it was published. *It* was the last one that I read in that way. I gave him a detailed critique on it, which he ignored. But I still sort of believe in what I said there, and that is the giant spider and its persuasiveness was the problem. What was most persuasive about the creature in *It* was that the monster appeared in the form of your deepest fear. If he could have somehow sustained that all the way to the end...

The writing in *It*—the picture of the group as kids and their interactions—was just marvelous writing, as good as Mark Twain. *The Shining* I like a lot, too. Actually, as you know, I've just recently published a piece on it. I wasn't as engaged by that book until I went back to it and reread it in preparation for writing the article. It holds together; it's got a classical sort of unity, working with the four characters. The movie gets in the way in some ways; I don't really like the movie. Kubrick is a very powerful director, and Nicholson is a very powerful actor, so images from the movie tend to get superimposed on the novel for me at least. I had to get away from the movie for a long time before I could really fully appreciate the qualities of the book.

JD: I think you also mentioned you liked *Misery* a lot.

BH: Yes. When Steve finished *Misery*, he said, "This is the best thing I've ever done." I think in some ways he still thinks that. I find it quite fine.

JD: What works would you pass over when evaluating King's enduring fiction? Why?

BH: *Firestarter* I've never really though much of. No one has ever quoted this, although I've told other people this from time to time:

when he published *The Stand*, he said to me, "This is my last effort
to really make it as a serious writer. If the critics will take this one
seriously, then that's the kind of writer I'll be." This is all
paraphrased, not exact, but I said to him, "If they don't take it
seriously, what kind of writer will you be?" He said, "I'll be a trash
writer." The critics didn't take it seriously, as you may know; there
weren't any reviews in *The New York Times Book Review* or things
like this. It sold well, but it was not treated as a contribution to
American literature when it was first published. He was very
disappointed by that. What came out of that disappointment was
Firestarter and *The Dead Zone*. He said to me at the time, "If I were
Graham Greene, I'd call these entertainments." He was really kind of
thinking of himself at the time as a writer who might write serious
novels and also kind of trashy, best-seller types to make money.

JD: From my reading, he had said that he thought *The Dead Zone*
was one of his best works.
BH: Well, what happened I think was he wrote it as an
entertainment, but then he did like it. Many people have told him
they think that's his best book. I don't agree. I think there's a big
problem in *The Dead Zone*, and that is I don't think that he really
understands politics. So his whole attempt to envision a political
career in America seems to me really not persuasive.

There is some very powerful stuff in *The Dead Zone*. I told him
once that I thought *The Dead Zone* was an autobiographical novel,
and he looked at me with considerable anger—he didn't like that
statement. I still think it's true in that it seems to me that this sense of
this person who's kind of cursed with this power parallels his
situation. It seems to me there's a series of stories in which he is
working with the writer as sort of a problematic kind of figure. It starts
with *'Salem's Lot*, actually, where there the writer is the person who
can go back and understand, know what's going on, and in some
way master it, although he can't stop it. But in *The Dead Zone*, the
writer is this person who has this gift that he can't really control, and
that makes him a figure that other people are just obsessed about.
That's the story of his life, isn't it? That's why I think it's
autobiographical, and you could go from that to *Misery* to *The Dark
Half*.

I still like *Cujo* a lot, as a naturalistic novel, really; it's not fantasy
or sci-fi or anything. The premise there is realism, and it proves he
can really write first-rate realism. He's proved that also in *The Body*
and some of the short novels, but I think *Cujo* works real well. He

doesn't think very much of it. When the movie versions of *Cujo* and *The Dead Zone* came out, he thought the movie version of *Cujo* was better than the novel, and he didn't think that about *The Dead Zone*. I would say almost the opposite. I think *Cujo* is a better novel than *The Dead Zone*, and the film of *The Dead Zone* is better than the film of *Cujo*.

JD: So are there any other works that you think are lacking? You mentioned you didn't care much for *The Tommyknockers*.
BH: No, I don't like *The Tommyknockers*, and I don't like *The Dark Half*. *The Tommyknockers* is the one that most bothered me because it was an attempt to do another big book; I mean, it's enormously long. It's got its moments, but the basic premise seems to me just wrong. It's inflated. Another book I like that has not gotten much attention is *Thinner*, and *The Dark Half* is sort of in that territory—it's not one of the big books. You can see if you look at his career that he's done big books and small books.

JD: *The Dark Half* sold a lot, but you're right: it wasn't a landmark in his career.
BH: No, and it's not that long. When I say big, I mean physically long. *The Dark Half* is a relatively short kind of idea book, like *Thinner*.

JD: Describe in your own words King's obsession with children and rites of passage.
BH: I think there are two things involved with it. One is that it's central to American literature, and he knows that. He read *Huckleberry Finn* and *The Hamlet* and *Winesburg, Ohio*.

He's also sort of a kid in some ways. Adolescence was a big moment in his life. I just saw this movie about these forty-year-old American businessmen who go off to a dude ranch—*City Slickers*. It was an enjoyable movie. But it also really does point to something in American life—the male bonding pattern, the notion that your most intense experiences are with your male gang in this immediate pre-adolescent period. When the guys on the trip are talking about the most memorable moments in their lives, one of them goes back to going to his first Yankees game with his dad. Steve is also hung up on baseball and the romance of baseball. I think the fact that he did not have a father in that stage is something that he's been compensating for his whole life. He feels he missed something absolutely central, and that is a male role model in that pre-adolescent moment. But I also think he made and had strong friendships. I mean it wasn't simply an absence that leads back to that moment but also warm friendships that he did form. I don't know who these people were, but I think he must have been part of a gang because he's a very gregarious guy; he makes friends easily. I can't see him as a lonely and isolated kid. I think he reached out to people, and they were responsive. So it's a pattern in American life; it's a pattern especially for him.

There's a lot of sexism involved in it. I think that learning to deal with women has been a very difficult pattern in his life. If you look at the female characters, you can see him really deliberately working at that issue. One reason I like *Cujo* is because I think he made a deliberate attempt there to create a heroic woman. It wasn't entirely successful, but he comes a long way to creating a female character who isn't just a kind of hanger-on to the boy gang. In *It* he regresses and gives us this token woman with the gang, but I accept it because that's the myth. There's a girl who joins the gang because she really isn't a girl; she's really a boy without a penis. But the thing I like about *It* is its willingness just to go with the myth there; it just plunges into it and says let's just live it through here and not worry about political correctness. I also think that is the limitation of that as a theme; what does it [the rites of passage theme] do with or for women? The woman is either tomboy or devouring monster. His best female characters tend to be devouring monsters; Annie Wilkes in *Misery* is probably his most memorable female character, and there again what he did was just pull out the stuff and say "Okay, I'm just going to create the absolutely most monstrous, frightening woman." But he also makes her sympathetic, which is really quite remarkable. We sort of half root for her. The movie really did that side of it quite well.

JD: Did King ever disclose to you the reason for dedicating *The Long Walk*, one of *The Bachman Books*, to you?
BH: I think it's because I read it and encouraged him at the time. The other people he dedicated it to were also people who were supportive and did encourage him as a student. He did do some rewriting before it was published. But basically, it's the book as he wrote it as a freshman.

He has said on several occasions that I influenced him. He tells a story that Douglas Winter quotes about me talking about *Soul on Ice*, which I did in fact teach in that modern American literature course. It was the Eldridge Cleaver book; I wanted a black book in there, and this was absolutely current stuff—it raised a lot of interesting issues. And he talks about me saying, "What about white soul?" Now I remember very clearly HIM doing this. As he read Cleaver's *Soul on Ice*, which is all about black soul, HE said "I want to write about white soul." So his belief that I influenced him in that respect seems to me quite wrong; that what he was doing was projecting on to me ideas that were in fact coming to him at that point. But I think the influence I did have on him was that I was knowledgeable about and involved with literature with a capital 'L,' but I did take his writing seriously. That is, I didn't compartmentalize it and say "This is trash; this isn't the real stuff." And that suggested I think to him that it is possible to have it both ways: to be a writer of literature and a writer with a mass audience.

JD: I would say that for the last two decades, King's fiction has had the greatest impact on the widest audience of any living author. I would also call it fair to say that present and future authors' success could be measured to King's. Do you see anyone surpassing him?
BH: Well, I don't know. I think he's set a precedent of the possibility of a writer who would bridge that gap between literature and mass culture. And others have pursued it. I think what made him so remarkable was the sheer inventiveness of the stuff he wrote from *Carrie* through *Misery*. It's quite astounding—the sheer number of new possibilities that he explored within that series of books and the sheer quantity of them—how many there were.

I do feel there's been some falling off in the quality since *Misery*. I also see some interesting stuff in some of the more recent work. So I'm not sure that that great period is over, but I think there's a possibility that it might be, and that this is not an uncommon kind of phenomenon. When you look at the history of writers, they don't necessarily manage to sustain a certain level of creativity for their whole lives.

I think in some ways though that both the strength and the limitation come from his identification with mass culture; that is, it would have been nice if he could have gotten a fuller education than he got. I think his reading is in certain ways limited. He's read enormous quantities of a certain kind of writing, and he does in that territory range around quite a bit. He reads people like Frank Norris, for example; Stephen Crane. But I think he could have learned a lot from European literature, for instance. I think it's perhaps unfortunate that, as far as I know, he hasn't done a really serious reading of the Russian novelists—Dostoyevsky and Tolstoy. So there are limitations in that respect. He is very much a writer within an American tradition. Just thinking maybe of some parallel cases, I think maybe Jack London and Steinbeck are good exemplars because they had the same kinds of limitations. They didn't really know world literature in some broad sense. They did know American culture and American literature and writing very thoroughly. But getting outside that American perspective, and looking into some of the kinds of issues that European writers in many ways have handled more fully than any Americans have—he's never done that, it seems to me: a limitation.

Once he said to me that one of the things about the contemporary period is that there is no dominant major novelist who is going to be regarded historically as the major novelist of our moment. There are some people who I think are doing very interesting writing now. Actually, the last time I was with him we talked about Thomas Pynchon. He's been interested in Pynchon for a long time. There are people like that who are in some ways more ambitious than he has ever been, and in some ways less ambitious. Again, his ambition has been to bridge the gap between mass culture and literature. Pynchon's ambition has been to write a GREAT book that will somehow really synthesize our sense of ourselves. I don't think that Steve really has a model of the great book in that sense in his head because it's largely a European model. It goes back to *War and Peace* or *The Brothers Karamazov* or *The Divine Comedy*. In many cases, those are books that he doesn't know.

JD: He's obviously become an icon in American pop-culture writing both in work and sales generated. You're saying you don't see anyone on the immediate horizon surpassing him.
BH: In that mode—as a kind of mass-cultural figure—I don't. And I don't really know the mass-culture mode that well to say. Somebody who's really coming on with as much fertility and inventiveness as he has had, I mean, I'm more likely to go back and say, well, here's Dickens or Jack London. Dickens had some of the same limitations that I was just talking about. He didn't really know traditional literature very well. He hadn't read *The Divine Comedy*, I don't think. He was too busy making a living, for one thing, and writing frantically in order to do that. He didn't have a sort of classical education as a background; neither did Jack London.

JD: Not since the time of William Shakespeare am I aware of a man who has produced so much material in the amount of time he's been writing. Just being in the Fogler Special Collections and seeing the boxes upon boxes of fiction King has donated keeps me in perpetual wonder. It would take me months to get through the material contained there, and the material there is only a little more than half of what he's written.

BH: Well, he is astoundingly productive. Most people—almost everybody—who's that productive is doing essentially formulaic writing. I accept your Shakespeare comparison, too. I teach Shakespeare. The thing that's constantly astounding to me about Shakespeare is the inventiveness of the non-formulaic characters; I mean, he's always coming up with a new way of dramatizing a situation. Every play is different, and that's what's mind-boggling. You can't even say, "Okay, here is the model of Shakespeare tragedy." Because the next Shakespeare tragedy you read is going to violate that model in some way. Shakespeare, like Dickens, was sort of a man-of-the-people kind of writer. Of course this is one reason why he [King] is interested in Faulkner, too: because Faulkner didn't have the classy education; he didn't make it through college, didn't get a thorough grounding in the masterpieces of western civilization.

JD: What's the extent of your communication with Stephen King right now?

BH: I see him maybe a couple times a year. Occasionally he calls me up and we talk a little bit. I wouldn't say it's an intimate friendship. I am hesitant to push it because I think he needs space. There's all of these people who want a piece of him. He's got to really define the terms of any relationship he has. We talk fairly regularly, and he seems to appreciate this fairly casual kind of interaction. He's likely to do something like call me up and invite me over to watch a movie or something.

JD: I've constructed a superficial model that I plan to use throughout my research. As not only a man who knows Stephen King and has consulted with him but also a person who's been involved in English for twenty-five years, if you were sitting before a board of English professors representing a high council of the U.S. English curriculum that was voting on a referendum deciding whether or not to allow King into the classroom and subsequently into the classic literature canon, what would your defense be on behalf of King?

BH: Well, first of all, since you asked Terry [Carroll Terrell] the same question, my sense of the whole nature of literature is quite different from his. He tends to think in terms of there are great geniuses who create great literature, and this happens because of the kind of personality or character they have, and this process will go on no matter what happens. Sooner or later, these great writers will be recognized, and he believes that Steve is one of them. His argument I think would basically be he's a great writer, period. My model is much more historically based. I think that the notion of literature as something that was kind of unique and precious and stands apart from mass culture is a phenomenon that developed starting somewhere around the middle of the nineteenth century. Let's say that kind of splitting process with certain kinds of writing validated as great or major or culturally significant and others seen as not culturally significant can be traced all the way back to the Renaissance. During the Renaissance, serious poets wrote in Latin, and Shakespeare couldn't possibly be a significant writer because he was writing in English. Academic people of the period believed that. That kind of discrimination has a long history behind it. It takes on particularly intense forms starting in the nineteenth century because of certain things that happened in capitalism within the period. That is, you do have the development of mass-production printing; mass-circulation magazines begin to appear; the newspaper as something that everyone reads is established; and there's a lot of money to be made out of writing, out of what once might have been thought of as art. As mass culture as a commercial phenomenon gets itself established as a place where big bucks can be made, there tends to be a split between that kind of cultural operation and other people who say "I don't want any part of that corrupt commercial process. I'm an artist, and an artist withdraws from that world and creates perfect texts or paintings." This person is totally indifferent to the marketplace. You have marketplace culture and you have museum culture in a sense, if you think of the museum as something else that also happens to literature. So that's the cultural situation that got itself established in the nineteenth century and has tended to continue on into the twentieth century. I think that Steve is an important figure in that history precisely because he declared that he wasn't satisfied with that split. He wasn't going to simply occupy one side or the other.

On the one hand, there have been a lot of people who are regarded as major writers who were very popular—Mark Twain, Charles Dickens, William Shakespeare. I think that there's another issue here, and that is that Steve's work really in some ways grows out of a conscious critique of that cultural split itself, and his critique of it is that what the split does is automatically write off everything that's on the popular culture side as mere commodity, trash, a contribution to the debased tastes of an illiterate mob. The high-culture people tend to look at the process that way. The people on the mass culture side look at those other folks and say, "Oh, they're just a bunch of snobs. They're not interested in communicating with ordinary human beings." Those are the two stereotypes you get, and he wants to critique both of them. As far as he succeeds in doing that, he also calls into question all of the ways in which we have traditionally thought about literature. He calls into question the very reality of the split. He in effect begins to force us to rethink the ways we think about a William Faulkner or a Jack London. That's happening. People among literary scholars and historians are in fact doing precisely that. They're starting to look again at writers who had been excluded from the canon on the grounds that they weren't serious writers. A classic example is *Frankenstein*, which has moved from the non-literary into one of the classics of literature in the last twenty years. We have a massive rethinking of the whole issue of canonicity and canonization; Steve's work is one of the forces that has initiated this rethinking of that issue.

IV. **Gary Hoppenstand**, Michigan State University. Dr. Hoppenstand received his Ph.D. in American Culture Studies from Bowling Green State University in 1985. He worked for one year as the curator of American Culture and Popular Culture collections at the Indiana State Museum in Indianapolis, Indiana, and he taught for several years in the English Department at the University of Toledo. Currently, he's an Associate Professor at MSU. He has instructed classes in composition, American literature and history, film studies, and television studies, and has a great interest in the study of popular culture, specifically popular literature. Aside from several other written projects on popular culture, including his most recent study, about Clive Barker, he has co-edited a book on Stephen King entitled *The Gothic World of Stephen King: Landscape of Nightmares* (Bowling Green State University Popular Press, 1987). Upon the completion of his work on Barker, he will resume writing a massive study of popular American best-selling horror-fiction writers called *Best-Selling Horrors: From Ira Levin to Stephen King.*

The following was a written interview conducted in October, 1991.

JD: What drew you to Stephen King's fiction in the first place?
GH: I was first attracted by Stephen King's fiction in the 1970s when I was working at a bookstore in Columbus, Ohio. I was in charge of ordering our selection of titles for the store, and thus I kept a close eye on what was selling. I paid no attention to the few hardcover copies we received from the then-unknown Stephen King, but when *Carrie*, *'Salem's Lot*, and *The Shining* were published in paperback, I—like thousands of others—was first hooked into reading them by their unusual, innovative cover illustrations. I particularly remember the all-black cover of *'Salem's Lot*, embossed with the face of a child vampire. It had no lettering on the front, and the only color to be seen was a single drop of red blood hanging from the corner of the vampire's mouth. It was indeed a truly striking production design for a paperback book at that time. Needless to say, once having read these three King novels, I was an unabashed fan for life.

JD: How does King's fiction relate to the Gothic tradition? What past writers draw the closest parallels with King?

161

GH: King is very much a part of the Gothic tradition in literature. Several years ago I wrote a book entitled *In Search of the Paper Tiger: A Sociological Perspective of Myth, Formula and the Mystery Genre in the Entertainment Print Mass Medium* (Bowling Green State University Popular Press, 1987) in which I defined the parameters of horror fiction. The same metaphoric ink that flowed in the blood of Walpole, Le Fanu, and Lovecraft now flows in the efforts of Stephen King. Yet, King's popularity is much greater than that of his predecessors. He has made the Gothic horror story today more accessible to a wider audience than it had been in the past, by appealing to new groups of readers, such as women and teenagers, readers who had, generally speaking, been passed over by earlier writers of Gothic fiction. I am, of course, not including the pseudo-Gothic as written by Ann Radcliffe in this discussion. Radcliffe and her following appealed primarily to women readers; she is more the forerunner of the modern romance novel than the modern horror novel. The Gothic novels that perhaps most influenced King's work include the "S"-authored classics of the genre, such as *Frankenstein* by Mary Wollstonecraft Shelley, *Dracula* by Bram Stoker, and *The Strange Case of Dr. Jekyll and Mr. Hyde* by Robert Louis Stevenson. A close reading of King's fiction reveals just how much these three novels impacted his writing in general. In addition, King himself has written eloquently and extensively of these important Gothic novels in his introduction to a Signet Classic omnibus edition that re-prints the three books, and in his fine book-length study of the horror genre in *Danse Macabre*. In fact, no other Gothic writer has opened herself or himself up for such close examination, figuratively speaking of course, as has King. He has not only provided a detailed rationale as to what makes him tick in *Danse Macabre*, but he has also provided the interested reader with a list and a detailed analysis of his favorite books in the genre.

JD: What do you suppose is the main reason King has been ignored by the academic world?

GH: The reasons why Stephen King has, for the most part, been ignored by academics are the same reasons why the horror genre as a whole has been ignored by academics. Both King and the horror genre are considered light entertainment, "mind candy." Academics perceive Stephen King and horror fiction as being unsophisticated, anti-intellectual, and crass. Of all forms of popular fiction—from the detective novel to the Western to science fiction—the horror story has historically been the least critically understood at the university.

Even with Edgar Allan Poe, who was arguably the finest American short story writer of the nineteenth century, it took the French to first recognize Poe's tremendous importance to American literature, and a number of American scholars today still resist giving Poe his due. Stephen King's fiction specifically has been attacked by academics as being too popular. There is an interesting suspicion among a number of professors that if an author writes best-selling fiction, then somehow that fiction is inferior to "less mainstream" efforts. Popularity itself is a clear indication of artistic weakness, the literary critic would argue, and is perceived as being diametrically opposite to quality. Personally, I have never entertained such a distinction. I do not condemn Charles Dickens or Mark Twain or Jack London because they were immensely popular authors. King is also criticized for being too prolific. The only author I know who is both prolific and critically appreciated is Joyce Carol Oates, and even she is not without her detractors who attempt to find fault in her productivity.

Finally, I think academics are suspicious of King because of his accessibility to the general reader. Academics like obscurity in their fiction. They like to take an author, like James Joyce, or a novel, like *Moby Dick*, and construct an elaborate analysis that explains what this author was really trying to say, or what the novel really represented. After all, academics are professionally condescending. They make a career of explaining literature to other less-educated folk. To deny complexity in fiction, to celebrate accessibility in literature: these things are anathema to university professors in search of validating what they do for a living. And when a novelist like Stephen King comes along who is not obscure, who doesn't require a Ph.D. in Literature from the University of Chicago to outline his scholarly significance, then it's entirely reasonable, and perhaps expected, when that author gets the critical cold shoulder at the academy.

JD: Even though you are an advocate of King's fiction, can you find anything about it that would support the academic world's doubts about it?
GH: Those things that disturb me about King's fiction are the same things that disturb me with Literature that is spelled with a capital "L." I sometimes find King to be long-winded, but I find the same fault with Tolstoy. I sometimes find King to be in need of stronger editorial guidance, but I find the same fault in James Fenimore Cooper. I sometimes find King to be overly conventional or formulaic, but I find the same fault in Dickens. In other words, those

areas of artistic weakness that exist in King's work exist in all fiction, great and small, and thus I think it intolerable when academics dismiss King as a serious writer because he is not perfect in a particular area, or in a particular skill. No author is divine. No author is perfect. I'm convinced that literary reputation is nothing more than an elaborate popularity contest. And I'm equally convinced that if an author, any author, strikes some sort of emotional or intellectual chord in the reader's soul, then that author is wonderful, marvelous, a wondersmith to be cherished.

JD: What types of responses have you received from your peers who are aware of your interest in King's fiction?

GH: I remember when my co-edited book entitled *The Gothic World of Stephen King: Landscape of Nightmares* was first published in 1987. I was then teaching in the English department at the University of Toledo, and, I believe, the only faculty member in that department to have a book published that year. For many of my peers, I was like the President of the United States who had just belched during an important speech; everyone respected the fact that I had just done something significant in publishing a book, but most were offended by the topic and tried to gracefully, or not-so-gracefully, dismiss it. I keep my research and my writings in the horror genre, and specifically my writings dealing with Clive Barker and Stephen King, mostly to myself, while I present to my superiors publications in more traditional areas, like early nineteenth-century American literature. I do the former for love, and the latter because I have to.

JD: The masses of people who don't read King are most often given their first dosage of his stories through film. While there are still millions of people who have read at least one King book, I have come upon a large number of people who have admitted never having read one but who had seen his film adaptations. With a few exceptions, King's films have often mutilated the richness of his texts, which film has a tendency to do by narrowing a complex story to ninety minutes of screen time. Do you feel King's film adaptations have been a major cause of the academic skeptics' refusal to accept King's work as serious? What are your feelings concerning the success or failure of King's stories on film?

GH: I can truthfully say that I never met a Stephen King novel or short story that I really and truly didn't like, and I can just as truthfully say that I've never met a movie based on a Stephen King story, except one, that I like. The movies *Carrie* and *The Dead Zone* are fair, but fair isn't good enough. The rest of the King cinematic batch is simply awful, except for *Stand By Me*, which by all accounts is a superior movie. For those who haven't read Stephen King, to judge him by Hollywood's interpretation of him (or lack of interpretation) is unfortunate, and does King a severe injustice. I think that part of the reason why King has failed to translate well onto the silver screen is because a two-hour movie denies the very strength of King's writing: complexity of character and plot. Stephen King is a novelist in the truest sense of the word. His narratives require time to unfold, to develop, to breathe. In a movie, we lose the nuance of King's subtle humor, his word play, his sense of verisimilitude. Slapping a two-hour restriction on the telling of *The Shining*, for example, is almost criminal, and the result is thus not unexpected. King simply does not translate well into motion pictures, and he has yet to recognize his own limitations in this area, as demonstrated by his occasional, regrettable forays into the cinematic realm, forays that produced such klunkers as *Maximum Overdrive*.

However, despite the array of motion-picture failures stemming from King's fiction, there still exists King's fiction itself. No matter how bad the movie is, the novels are sitting there on the bookshelf, unchanged, waiting to be opened, to be read, to be enjoyed.

JD: Before I ask you to answer my own questions concerning what I found in King's fiction during my research, I would like to know what you think are his most predominant and significant themes.

GH: Regarding the significant themes that appear in King's fiction, I have dealt with several of what I perceive to be the more important ones in my introduction to *The Gothic World of Stephen King*, entitled "The Horror of It All: Stephen King and the Landscape of the American Nightmare." The real horror in a number of King's stories is shown to be some type of family break-up or some type of romantic discord, and King frequently employs supernatural horror to frame psychological terror, as perhaps best illustrated in *The Shining, Pet Sematary*, and *The Dead Zone*.

Another theme that King frequently employs is the notion of adolescent alienation. Young people are often persecuted in King's novels, and as these young people struggle against society, or against their peers, or against some supernatural force, they strive to discover an identity. King has worked most frequently, and most successfully, with adolescent alienation. His novels *Carrie*, *'Salem's Lot*, *The Shining*, *Firestarter*, *Christine*, *The Talisman* (with Peter Straub), and especially *It*, all feature young protagonists who are tormented by society or by family, who are isolated yet still resilient, and who endeavor to survive in a hostile, ugly world.

King also enjoys using adolescent revenge fantasies in his fiction. For example, in *Carrie* and *Christine*, Stephen King features an introverted adolescent character (or more correctly, a whimpy nerd) who is in possession of a great, supernatural power, yet who is also the object of ridicule and scorn among peers because he or she is "different." After discovering and nurturing their secret power, these persecuted teenagers become, in turn, the persecutors of their former tormentors.

Stephen King has also consistently toyed with apocalyptic, or end of the world, ideas as seen in his novels *The Stand*, *It*, the "Dark Tower" series, and in the long short story (or short novel) "The Mist."

Finally, I've recently noticed a new trend in King's writings, in which he has an author protagonist who appears to be a thinly veiled version of himself, and who undergoes a desperate (and deadly) search for a self-identity. These seeming autobiographical investigations into the nature of writing and being a writer, such novels as *Misery* and *The Dark Half*, are among the most interesting in King's literary canon. They reveal his love/hate attitudes regarding his success as a best-selling author, on the one hand, and with his artistic failure at being typecast as a brand-name gore master on the other.

JD: How do you feel King interprets the moral standing of contemporary American society? Does he see much hope in the power of good or does he see the majority of Americans as being the embodiments of immorality with the intent of persecuting both their subjective and objective worlds?

GH: Stephen King is a difficult author to pigeonhole, and this is one of his greatest strengths as a writer. In several of King's tales, he does indeed portray the triumph of good over evil, the re-establishment of moral virtue over moral corruption. The novel *It*, for example, nicely defines the total defeat of evil, as represented in the destruction of the spider-Eater-of-Worlds-Pennywise-the-Clown creature. Yet, "The Mist," written by the very same author, presents a grimly pessimistic view of humanity's fate (though King is not a total nihilist in the story; he does provide his reader with a small measure of hope, however meager, in the end). Certainly the most complex King novel dealing with moral issues is the apocalyptic *The Stand*, which is King's contribution to the epic quest narrative. The huge cast of characters in *The Stand* (as well as the novel's massive length) allows King to construct a variety of good and evil personalities. These characters run the breadth of the moral spectrum, and in a sense, despite the fantastic events in the story, they are quite emblematic of the human condition as it actually exists. *The Stand*, in my opinion, is not only one of Stephen King's great artistic triumphs, I think it is one of the finest fantasy novels ever written. Period.

JD: What do you think King suggests as a remedy for a blemished human moral condition? In other words, how can a human overcome his or her human flaws?

GH: There is much in the work of Stephen King that reflects a 1960s/70s mindset. He is often suspicious of powerful governmental bureaucracies, such as seen in his novel *Firestarter* and in his television mini-series *Golden Years*. King is also critical of right-wing religious fanaticism, as seen in *Carrie* with Carrie White's mother. And thus, regarding the issue of moral condition, I see King advocating in a number of his characters an inward search for truth and moral strength. Outside the individual, in the realm of Church and State, there lurks danger, even death. King's view of bureaucracy is perhaps even paranoid in its intensity. Inwardly, however, a person can find hope in the face of hopelessness, success in the face of adversity. In one of King's more apocalyptic novels, *It*, the children protagonists (and later, the childlike adults), defeat a monolithic, pervasive evil by discovering an inner strength, a faith in oneself potent enough to better that all-powerful evil.

JD: Why do you think King is so concerned with adolescence and rites of passage? Why are a bulk of his texts centered on individual children or groups of children being persecuted by their adult worlds?

GH: One reason I suspect that King is so concerned with children and their rites of passage into adulthood in his work, and I'm only guessing at this having no solid proof in hand, is because King views his writing as a cathartic act, a purging of his own personal phobias. Writing, for Stephen King, is like confession. He purges himself by confessing himself. From some small gleanings of King's personal life, and some reading between the lines from his comments, I think King in several of his novels and short stories is resolving tensions he himself experienced in his youth. The persecuted adolescent, the ravenous bully, the nerd who is out of step with his peers: these, I imagine, are all images from King's childhood, and in the elaborate fictional world that he invents in his fiction, he creates a situation where the persecuted adolescent discovers an inner strength, where the ravenous bully gets his just deserts, and where the nerd makes peers fear his or her immense power.

JD: Would you classify King as a Romanticist? His belief that returning to observe childhood experiences from a mature perspective resulting in a completion of an emotional wheel—an achievement of human wholeness—seems to imply that he is. Is he also a naturalist?

GH: One has to be a bit careful when attaching labels such as "Romanticist" or "Naturalist" to King's writings, because they are mutually exclusive concepts. In their book entitled *Literary Terms: A Dictionary* (Noonday Press, 1989), Karl Beckson and Arthur Ganz define "Romanticism" as "...the characteristics of romances, or fanciful stories, whose extravagances carried pejorative connotations...a kind of exotic landscape which evoked feelings of pleasing melancholy." Certainly, all of horror fiction in general, and King's fiction specifically, fall into this category. Beckson and Ganz define "Naturalism" as the "doctrine that holds that all existent phenomena are in nature and thus within the sphere of scientific knowledge; it maintains that no supernatural realities exist." Thus, though elements of Naturalism may appear in King's work, he most certainly is not part of the Naturalist school.

JD: How has King created a bridge between popular and classic culture?

GH: Not yet, but the bridge is getting closer to being completed. In the past ten years, I have seen more and more academics recognize in King elements of literary quality. Yet, these academics are but a handful when compared to the overall literary establishment that still perceives in King the "penny dreadful" pot-boiler, the hack writer.

JD: How does King feel about the advanced state of American technology? Does he believe it is good in its furtherance of the human condition, or does he see it as being a curse? How does he illustrate humans' relationship with their machines and inventions?

GH: These questions attempt to elicit an either/or response, and I would advance the notion that King goes both ways. In some of his writings, such as in "The Mist," King sees evil in technology; in other writings, such as in "The Langoliers" from *Four Past Midnight* (where the jet airliner is the instrument of escape and salvation) King is either ambivalent about technology, or simply does not view it as a threat to the human condition.

JD: If King does present a negative portrait of American technology, what does he provide as an alternate solution to the technological advance that tends to make slaves of its masters? Is there a solution?

GH: Using my above example of the short novel (or the long short story) entitled "The Mist," which is one of my favorite King stories, technology brings the downfall of civilization as we know it. King nicely describes the particulars of this apocalyptic event off-stage, out-of-sight, hence leaving his reader to focus on the devastating particulars of the awful here and now. The apocalypse is thus brought down to size, made more understandable—and more frightening—because a small group of victims must deal with their "brave new world." In King's stories where he has technology as the great bogey man, there is no solution to its evil. Technology, as Stephen King sees it in "The Mist," is a Pandora's Box that should not be opened, but when it is unfortunately opened by foolish people (in particular, by foolish scientists, one of King's favorite stereotypes), then it does not disappear with a wave of the brave knight's lance. Once released, technology-as-evil cannot be put back into the Box.

JD: King's fiction often emphasizes the subordination of the individual for the sake of larger society. Often his characters are swallowed by a society demanding conformity. What point is King trying to make? Is he an anti-social in favor of an anarchist state, or is he merely trying to illustrate that all humans are trapped in a great societal machine from which there is no escape?

GH: I think that this question is asking for a more complex question than what's really there in King's work. Indeed, a goodly quantity of noble characters are sacrificed during the course of a number of Stephen King stories, but I think King is using these characters in a more formulaic, less philosophical, way. I don't mean this to be taken as a criticism of King's efforts; rather, I perceive King as the master storyteller who is able to effectively use every one of his many literary tools to entertain us. Formulaically speaking, characters are sacrificed in horror fiction, not to advance some larger political or philosophical ideology, but rather they are killed off to demonstrate just how evil Evil is, to show that moral triumph is often bought at a terrible price. Lovable, sympathetic characters bite the big one in King because he wants to seduce us into the story. He wants us to become involved with the trials of a protagonist, then when the protagonist is killed, we are outraged, horrified at losing such a good friend, and we quickly turn the page to see what happens next. This technique, or literary gimmick, is not King's alone. Read mid-way through Dan Simmon's wonderful horror novel *Summer of Night* and you'll see exactly what I mean.

JD: How does King observe the typical American nuclear family? Is it a vehicle of love and nurturance, or is it a vehicle of repression and destruction? Is this a realist portrayal? If so, how does this point of view link him to significant writers of the past?

GH: I tend to view King's use of the family in his work in a pessimistic light. I am reminded of his "Children of the Corn" short story from his *Night Shift* collection, or his novel *The Shining*, where the evil that confronts the family is not just supernatural in nature; it is also profoundly psychological. The greatest scare in *The Shining*, for example, comes not so much from the haunted Overlook Hotel itself, as from the deranged, psychopathic father, Jack Torrance, and his ravenous attacks against his wife, Wendy, and his son, Danny. *The Shining* is a classic tale of family abuse doctored up as a ghost story. And if one senses in King, as I do, a sympathy to child abuse or wife abuse, then this highlights his work as being very contemporary, very in-touch with current national and local newspaper headlines. Of course, most of the classic Gothic fiction of the past several hundred years features women in peril as a motif of the formula. Remember all of those paperback Gothic romance book covers from the 1960s and 1970s where the imposing image of a castle (with just a single light ominously glowing in one window) seems to threaten some beautiful, young female while she's running away from the edifice in her luminous white nightgown? Now that's a popular-culture icon if ever there was one! But King seems to put a contemporary, distinctly American twist to this Gothic motif into his novels and short stories. One senses in *The Shining* that the Torrance family is representative of why the divorce rate in America is so high and is also representative of our ever-unfolding understanding of family violence and its catastrophic effects on women and children.

JD: How does King deal with stereotypes? Is he above his contemporaries in trying to include minorities—women, children, blacks, the elderly—as stealthy, autonomous individuals, or is he still guilty of either discluding them or not making them as powerful as their white male counterparts? How does King's treatment of minorities connect him with other significant writers like Faulkner, O'Connor, and Twain?

GH: King is not above employing stereotypes in his writings, but on the whole I would say that he is very cognizant of using nonstereotypical minority characters. Both women and blacks figure prominently in several of his novels and short stories. However, drawing a connection to Faulkner, O'Connor, and Twain, is, at best, a risky proposition since this supposed connection baits the issue of presentism. Each of these authors was very much part of his or her time and place in history, and thus their respective, and differing, treatments of minorities are framed by the era in which they lived. By the same token, King is very much an American author of the period from the 1970s to the present. King has had the benefit of knowing about the Civil Rights movement of the 1960s that the others did not. King has had the benefit of knowing about the ERA movement of the 1970s that the others did not. Thus, though all four fine writers may view with sympathy minorities, the all-important specifics of that sympathy are quite different.

JD: What does King suggest to humanity when calling up weapons of survival in the shadow of adversities?

GH: King takes survival very seriously. His characters are often put through the most heinous of situations before they escape their tormentors and triumph. I am reminded, in particular, of writer Paul Sheldon's trials in *Misery* and how Sheldon uses the instrument of his love and of his torment, the typewriter, as a physical weapon against his tormentor, Annie Wilkes. It's an ironic gesture on King's part, and wonderfully humorous in a grim way. In effect, Paul Sheldon has to come to grips with his greatest love and his greatest hate in pursuit of survival.

JD: Will King be taken seriously in this generation, or will he follow the pattern of his literary predecessors and find his critical acclaim with the next generation, possibly after he has passed away? If this is your prediction of the future, why does this postmortem recognition tend to be the trend?

GH: I think King is becoming critically recognized more and more as time goes on, and I also think that he will find a grudging acceptance during his lifetime, though it will be the same type of acceptance that Charles Dickens received before he died. During Dicken's prolific literary career, people—both critics and readers alike—saw in him something special, though it took his death and a generation or two before he was totally accepted. Some authors never make the final leap into the college lit course, and only time will tell if I'm right about King's chances.

JD: What about King's fiction has attracted its mass following?

GH: King has so effectively attracted his mass following because he has appealed to the two more important groups of readers: women and adolescents. King appeal has not limited itself to gender- or age-specific audiences. Tom Clancy and Westerns sell to men but not women. Romances appeal to women and not men. Science fiction appeals to the young more than the old. King does well with all groups. Lacking any specific publishing statistics, I draw upon my experience as a bookstore clerk and as an educator for ten years when I say that I have seen all types of readers with a Stephen King book in hand, and this is a real tribute to his skill as a popular storyteller.

JD: What separates King from other writers respected in the horror genre, like Clive Barker, Peter Straub, or Dean Koontz? With the possible exception of Koontz, why does King's brand of fiction outsell his contemporaries in the field?

GH: King is different from Clive Barker and Peter Straub in that he is less a writer of literature (as are Barker and Straub) and more a storyteller from the oral tradition. In a recent telephone conversation with Clive Barker, we discussed King's popularity, and Clive made the profound remark that King seems to be very intimate with his readers, that what he lacked in literary polishing he more than made up for in his effective use of a conversational tone. King is more the friend telling a good, scary tale, and less the nouveau stylist, intellectually exploring new territories of literature. Of course such intimacy requires less literary sophistication and more sensitivity to satisfying the immediate requirements of a mass reading audience. King, like his nearest selling rival, Dean Koontz, is closely attuned to his reader's expectations. They both deliver what their readers want from them: to be entertained with a minimum of effort.

JD: What substance do you see in King's popular fiction that differentiates him from his fellow best-sellers—Tom Clancy, Jackie Collins, Danielle Steele, and V.C. Andrews?

GH: For the most part, King is different from his fellow best-selling peers in the complexity of his storytelling. He is indeed a "brand name author" (a term invented by King to describe how the top authors in the book industry operate) like Collins, Steele, and Andrews, and he consciously produces what he thinks his readers expect from him. Unlike his "mental fluff" fellow authors, King does what he does with great complexity. He writes epics, while the others write fluff. He is articulate and well-informed about his craft, as demonstrated by his non-fiction study of the horror genre, *Danse Macabre*, and though he accommodates his readers' expectations, he is able to effectively write a protest of his situation, as he did in both *Misery* and *The Dark Half* (books that no other best-selling writer would have the ability to write) that both is critical of the industry and entertaining at the same time. Stephen King, as a storyteller, is in a category by himself.

JD: Does King's fiction have the backbone to make it worthy of inclusion in an academic canon? If so, why?

GH: Yes it does, and if for no other reason than what I mentioned in the last response: that King is a complex, yet entertaining, author. With the exception of Clive Barker's later novels (which are the best in the genre) and Robert McCammon's *Swan Song*, and some of what Brian Lumley has done recently, horror fiction writers do not write epics. Horror writers are more concerned with effect, with shock, with a quick scare that reminds their readers that the $5.00 or $6.00 spent on the latest TOR book is not wasted. It's hard to maintain THE SCARE over the course of a thousand pages. Complexity of plot and character development: these seem to be the twin literary adversaries of the typical paperback gore master. Yet King has written not one, but two epics of the genre, *The Stand* and *It*, that are like the *War and Peace* of the horror genre. These two books alone will secure King's reputation as one of the best twentieth-century horror fiction authors because of their depth and richness.

JD: What Stephen King books are your favorites, and why do they work for you? What about them makes them in your eyes the best manifestations of his talent?

GH: In addition to *The Stand* and *It*, my favorite King books include *'Salem's Lot*, a novel that, along with Robert McCammon's *They Thirst*, is one of the best vampire novels written in the past twenty-five years, and also *Pet Sematary*, in which King seems to effectively target humanity's oldest, most profound fear: one's anxiety of death and death's aftermath.

JD: What King books don't work for you? What in content are these books lacking that qualified your favorites? Why don't they work?

GH: King's weakest novels include *The Tommyknockers*, in which he doesn't seem to know what he's doing with the story, and *Carrie*, in which he is still learning to flex his young literary muscles. The narrative structure of *Carrie* makes it one of King's weaker novels, though the novel's characters are very interesting. All in all, I would rather be reading "weak" Stephen King than reading the "strong" efforts of other best-selling authors.

JD: Do you feel King is often guilty of overpursuing an issue? Does he sometimes suffer from elephantitis of the text?

GH: I don't think that King overpursues any particular issue, but I do think that he is in need of stronger editorial supervision from time to time. Because of his great commercial success in recent years, King is given a freedom that few other authors enjoy: a greater control over the final product of his writing. And I don't know if this is necessarily a good thing. I suppose that all writers require some type of help at certain moments, and King is no exception. However, I also think that King's rambling, often loosely structured, writing style suits him well. It supports that sense of immediacy with his reader that Clive Barker correctly identifies. I also think that King sometimes spends too much time establishing his setting. For example, nearly the entire first half of *The Shining* is stage-setting, and it's only the second half of the book which makes it a real treat to read.

JD: If you were asked to speak your opinion on behalf of including King into the presently accepted literary canon by a group of English professors representing the U.S. English curriculum, what would be your defense of King? What would people gain from having his fiction introduced into the classroom?

GH: Great literature does three crucial things. It, first, effectively deals with, or reveals, some significant aspect of the human condition. It, second, allows its reader to be emotionally or intellectually uplifted, to learn something new of life, to become thoroughly involved with characters or with a story that subsequently has some important meaning for the reader. And it, finally, must survive the "test of time." It must not be overly topical in its appeal. King, I think, has fulfilled the first two requirements for great literature, and only time will tell if he accomplishes the third.

JD: Do you suppose King's disclusion from the canon has been better for him in his attitude toward completing a work of fiction, or do you suppose that inclusion would activate a mental reaction in him causing him to write fiction with even richer substance because of the class it would put him in?

GH: Oh boy, I always get a bit squeamish when I try to get inside an author's head to such an extent as to attempt to answer this question. Only King himself would be able to truthfully reply to an issue involving some aspect of a personal "mental reaction."

JD: What might readers expect from King in the future? With the end of Castle Rock in his recent book, *Needful Things*, King has said goodbye to an important realm of his fiction. Will King continue to write horror, or will he more openly experiment with different devices of fiction as he did in *Four Past Midnight*, which contains a science-fiction tale and a psychological thriller devoid of supernatural interference? Might readers expect a new era of King fiction?

GH: I have waited for years to see if Stephen King will leave the horror genre, and each new book that he publishes convinces me more that he never will depart from the horror genre. Instead, he will do as you suggested he did in his recent *Four Past Midnight* collection, and that is to investigate further the many varieties and sub-formulas that are to be found in the horror genre, like the science-fiction tale or the psychological thriller, and so on. I am not one of those readers who think that because King writes nothing other than horror fiction, that he is an inferior author. The vast majority of what Louis L'Amour wrote was the same, yet this did not disqualify him as an important American author of the frontier. King obviously feels comfortable doing what he does because he does it so often and so well. If there is "a new era of King fiction" looming on the horizon, then I hope that it's much the same as the old era. I can't really see King writing mainstream sex, money, and power novels, nor can I see him writing high-tech spy thrillers (though elements of both formulas do appear in King's own work). Instead, I think King has found an artistic voice that fits him nicely.

JD: Do you feel King will mature as a writer as he grows older, or has he worn his material thin?

GH: King has greatly matured as a writer since the publication of his first novel, *Carrie*. And over the past decade and a half, King has continued to improve his craft. He has been a prolific writer, but he has always seemed to discover new ways of doing things, new ways of scaring the beejesus out of us, new ways of commenting upon the human condition. If his act hasn't worn thin by now, I don't expect it to in the near future. At least, I hope it doesn't, because I think Stephen King has been good to us. He has been good to those many adolescent readers who otherwise would never crack open a book, let alone read it. He has been good for the horror genre, bringing to it a greater sense of integrity, respect, and commercial success (and it's hard to argue with success). He has been good to me, providing me many hours of reading pleasure. Stephen King is truly one of a kind.

Works Cited

Bare Bones: *Conversations on Terror with Stephen King*. Eds. Tim Underwood and Chuck Miller. New York: Warner Books, 1988.

Barker, Clive. "Surviving the Ride." *Kingdom of Fear: The World of Stephen King*. Eds. Tim Underwood and Chuck Miller. New York: New American Library, 1986: 55-63.

Bosky, Bernadette Lynn. "The Mind's A Monkey: Character and Psychology in Stephen King's Recent Fiction." *Kingdom of Fear: The World of Stephen King*. Eds. Tim Underwood and Chuck Miller. New York: New American Library, 1986: 211-37.

Gallagher, Bernard J. "Reading Between the Lines: Stephen King and Allegory." *The Gothic World of Stephen King: Landscape of Nightmares*. Eds. Gary Hoppenstand and Ray B. Browne. Bowling Green, Ohio: Bowling Green State University Popular Press, 1987: 37-48.

Hatlen, Burton. "Good and Evil in Stephen King's *The Shining*." *"The Shining" Reader*. Ed. Tony Magistrale. Washington: Starmont House, 1990: 81-103.

Indick, Ben P. "King and the Literary Tradition of Horror and the Supernatural." *Fear Itself: The Horror Fiction of Stephen King*. Eds. Tim Underwood and Chuck Miller. San Francisco: Underwood-Miller Publishers, 1982: 153-67.

King, Stephen. *The Aftermath*. Special Collections Department, Raymond H. Fogler Library, University of Maine at Orono.

____. *Blaze*. Special Collections Department, Raymond H. Fogler Library, University of Maine at Orono.

____. "The Body." *Different Seasons*. New York: Viking Penguin, 1982.

____. "The Boogeyman." Special Collections Department, Raymond H. Fogler Library, University of Maine at Orono.

____. *Christine*. New York: Viking Press, 1983.

____. "Culch." Special Collections Department, Raymond H. Fogler Library, University of Maine at Orono.

____. *Danse Macabre*. New York: Everest House Publishers, 1981.

____. *Firestarter.* New York: Viking Press, 1980.

____. *Four Past Midnight.* New York: Viking Penguin, 1990.

____. *Needful Things.* New York: Viking Penguin, 1991.

____. *Night Shift* (Original Typescript). Special Collections Department, Raymond H. Fogler Library, University of Maine at Orono.

____. *'Salem's Lot.* New York: Signet New American Library, 1975.

____. *The Stand: The Complete and Uncut Edition.* New York: Doubleday, 1990.

____. "Your Kind of Place." Special Collections Department, Raymond H. Fogler Library, University of Maine at Orono.

Magistrale, Tony. *Landscape of Fear: Stephen King's American Gothic.* Bowling Green, Ohio: Bowling Green State University Popular Press, 1988.

____. *The Moral Voyages of Stephen King.* Washington: Starmont House, 1989: 44-55.

____. *Stephen King, The Second Decade*: Danse Macabre *to* The Dark Half. New York: Twayne, 1992.

Newhouse, Tom. "A Blind Date with Disaster: Adolescent Revolt in the Fiction of Stephen King." *The Gothic World of Stephen King: Landscape of Nightmares.* Eds. Gary Hoppenstand and Ray B. Browne. Bowling Green, Ohio: Bowling Green State University Popular Press, 1987: 49-56.

Notkin, Deborah. "Stephen King: Horror and Humanity For Our Time." *Fear Itself: The Horror Fiction of Stephen King.* Eds. Tim Underwood and Chuck Miller. San Francisco: Underwood-Miller Publishers, 1982: 131-44.

Schuman, Samuel. "Taking Stephen King Seriously: Reflections on a Decade of Best Sellers." *The Gothic World of Stephen King: Landscape of Nightmares.* Eds. Gary Hoppenstand and Ray B. Browne. Bowling Green, Ohio: Bowling Green State University Popular Press, 1987: 107-14.

Smith, Stevie. "To Carry the Child." *The Norton Anthology of Modern Poetry: Second Edition.* New York: W.W. Norton and Company, 1988: 652-60.

Winter, Douglas. *Stephen King: The Art of Darkness.* New York: New American Library, 1984.

____. *Stephen King.* Washington: Starmont House, 1982.

Yarbro, Chelsea Quinn. "Cinderella's Revenge—Twists on Fairy Tale and Mythic Themes in the Work of Stephen King." *Fear Itself: The Horror Fiction of Stephen King.* Eds. Tim Underwood and Chuck Miller. San Francisco: Underwood-Miller Publishers, 1982: 45-56.

Index